Archival Information Processing for
Sound Recordings: The Design of a Database
for the Rodgers & Hammerstein Archives
of Recorded Sound

by David H. Thomas

MLA Technical Report No. 21
Music Library Association
1992

The Music Library Association

P.O. Box 487, Canton, MA 02021

ISSN: 0094-5099

ISBN: 0-914954-45-8

MLA Technical Reports
Series Editor
Richard P. Smiraglia

Library of Congress Cataloging in Publication Data
Thomas, David H. (David Hayward), 1962–
    Archival information processing for sound recordings : the design of a database for the Rodgers & Hammerstein Archives of Recorded Sound / by David H. Thomas.
    p. cm. —(MLA technical report, ISSN 0094-5099 : no. 21)
Includes index.
ISBN 0-914954-45-8
    1. Sound recording libraries—New York (N.Y.)   2. Cataloging of sound recordings—Data processing.   3. Archives, Audio-visual—New York (N.Y.)   4. Data base design.   5. Rodgers and Hammerstein Archives of Recorded Sound.   I. Title.   II. Series: MLA technical reports : no. 21.
ML111.5.T5   1992   92-5551
025.3'482—dc20   CIP
                                                                MN

Contents

CONTENTS

CONTENTS

List of Figures

Foreword

Every collection of recorded sound serves a basic purpose: to educate, enlighten, and entertain a constituency. Private collections serve mainly collectors and those in their immediate circles; school collections support curricula. Many of these needs are met by mass-marketed, commercial recordings. When the recordings are no longer useful or desirable, the collection can be sold, traded, or discarded with relative impunity.

Those collections called archives, however, serve an additional purpose—to preserve the cultural heritage of recorded sound in order to educate, enlighten, and entertain a future, and perhaps presently unknown, constituency. Archives also carry the responsibility to preserve and maintain those recorded products of artistic endeavor that were never made available to the public through commercial release. These specialized recordings often are made on particularly fragile, perishable media, with little or no documentation of their production or provenance. It is up to the archives to capture what is known about these recordings, as well as what is on them, before it is lost forever. Most archives exist in the academic world, where their constituencies are relatively stable and focused. Access to the collection is limited to those who belong to the institution and those who have made special arrangements to use it. Collection development and preservation can be carried out along the lines of the institution's curriculum goals, and assumptions made about those who will need to use the materials.

The Rodgers and Hammerstein Archives of Recorded Sound, however, is unique in that its constituency is vast—almost unknowable; it is one of the few sound archives open to the public without qualification. Certain segments of the arts community are expected: professional musicians, music critics, discographers, actors, performing arts students, and media professionals. Other users are less predictable: students of all disciplines and from hundreds of institutions, historians, market researchers, retirees, and siblings and children of those who hold a certain vintage recording special in their heart. For these, almost any preserved example of recorded sound might hold special meaning and value.

The easy part has always been to collect. Those involved in recording sound have always come to R&H to store and maintain their intellectual products for the future. How best to do that, given the limited resources of the public library, has always been a challenge. Standard library cataloging, although it would provide the access points necessary for this material, is too time-consuming for the myriad items contained in these collections of private recordings, demo records, unique reel tapes, and other noncommercial sound carriers.

But standard archival practice, which uses limited access points leading to a register of the contents of a collection where one scans the individual listings, is also unsatisfactory. Researchers who use recorded sound are most often in search of a specific piece of music, a specific performer or speaker, or a dated performance, which may not exist in recorded form except for a concert performance or other noncommercial source. Cataloging at R&H has to point to each of these pieces individually and directly, even if the user does not know of the existence of, or the scope of, a collection.

David Thomas's work on the sound recordings database has been an evolving process of serving each need in turn, while avoiding the duplication of data entry. Most valuable has been the search engine of the database, which allows the curator and reference librarians to search across all collections at once to answer patron requests for works of recorded sound that do not exist, or are not in the archives' collections, in commercial form.

The database has helped turn chaos into order, "stuff in a box" into processed collections, curator's memory into printed finding aids, miscellaneous re-taping into systematic preservation routines, and labor-intensive scanning of archival registers into quick and easy computer searching. What's more, it allows data on incoming material to be entered in rudimentary form, tracked, added to, edited, completed, and printed without duplication of effort. Its power and flexibility have allowed us to serve our constituency within the strictures of limited time and resources.

In a larger sense, the database serves as a model for other sound archives, which, although they may never adopt its structure or its software in particular, will benefit from its concept of unified data management for the acquisition, cataloging, and preservation of noncommercial sound collections. With the ever-increasing cooperative efforts of the sound archives community through organizations such as the Associated Audio Archives Committee of the Association for Recorded Sound Collections, it is hoped that this type of data might even be shared across local- and wide-area computer networks in the future.

CHRISTINE HOFFMAN
ASSISTANT CHIEF
RODGERS & HAMMERSTEIN ARCHIVES
OF RECORDED SOUND
THE NEW YORK PUBLIC LIBRARY FOR THE
PERFORMING ARTS

Preface

Fresh out of library school in 1987, I joined the staff at the Rodgers & Hammerstein Archives. I was hired to work on a special grant-funded project to catalog the noncommercial sound recordings collections at the Archives. At the time I didn't see myself as a professional who was particularly interested in sound recordings in libraries and archives; cataloging sound recordings simply was the best option open to me at the time. Of course I have my own record collection at home, and I am personally interested in music, but I didn't have any special feelings or any important drive to work with sound recordings in a library setting. I didn't identify personally with sound recordings. Nor did I really consider the use of archival descriptive techniques for sound recordings to be an area of interest to me.

Instead, it seemed to me that the job might raise a certain number of interesting complications that would enable me to derive greater satisfaction upon completing the work at hand. I did not foresee getting as involved in the sound recordings and archives fields as I subsequently have. But I have gotten deeply involved in this stuff; the issues of what and how to describe sound recordings that are archival in nature turn out to be extremely fascinating.

The database that is described in this report did not arise as a pre-planned creation. When I started at the Archives, my only concern was to give some manner of access to the materials assigned to me for description. To that end I followed practices that I had learned for describing archival materials—I created finding aids and cataloged the collections described in those finding aids. However, the staff at the Archives felt it was important for us to provide as much information as possible about individual recordings within a collection—regardless of the ultimate size that any finding aid might reach. As I typed my way through a number of finding aids of increasing length, I found myself getting more and more frustrated at the fact that I had to re-type a lot of the same information, and that the information was largely inflexible after it was input.

At some stage in this process, my colleague at R&H, Gary Gisondi, made the suggestion that I might want to explore using a database-management software package to capture the information that I had been typing into a word processor, from which I could then output finding aids. At first I tried simply to capture the same sort of information in the database program that I had captured in the word processor. However, once I had been working with the database program for a while, I found myself trying to get the system to do even more. As time passed the application grew to encompass a larger number of the technical and descriptive processes required of archival sound recordings materials.

Like the database itself, this report was unplanned and grew from innocent beginnings. In 1988, Richard Smiraglia asked me to write an article discussing how we at the Archives cataloged sound recordings using archival methods. While I was writing that article, Richard thought that some of what I was describing could be useful to others in the profession, but it was not appropriate for the article on archival processing. He suggested that I write a report describing the database in detail, and I agreed.

The database has proved to be quite useful to a wide variety of people at the Archives, as well as elsewhere in the New York Public Library. Those of us who actually describe these materials find that the time needed to describe a collection is drastically reduced; the staff have described nearly 20,000 unique items in only six and a half staff-years. Sound engineers creating preservation transfer copies of these materials find that they can quickly locate specific items and create necessary documentation rapidly with this system. Reference staff and users of the Archives can locate and identify materials in the collections that were wholly unavailable previously. Finally, the system has been successfully installed at a second location in the New York Public Library system, where it is being used to process archival moving image materials. For these reasons, this database has been very important to the New York Public Library and its users.

I hope that a description of the database will prove to be useful to others in the archives and music library fields. It is my hope that this report will help other professionals avoid some of the more alluring (but falsely beneficial) options that we tried in the early stages. I also hope that this report will raise some questions about the types of data that information professionals track and how best that information can be stored and retrieved. Ultimately, it would be gratifying to see this report inspire further development of relational databases for information storage and retrieval in the archival and library fields.

Contents of the Report

This report is organized into five chapters and two appendixes. The first chapter contains a discussion of the theoretical underpinnings of the database and a description of its development. The focus of this chapter is a discussion of the fundamental differences between archival and bibliographic descriptive techniques as they apply to sound recordings. The second chapter contains a description of R&H and an account of the evolution of the information-gathering process for noncommercial sound recordings, starting with word-processed finding aids and ending with the relational database application, paying attention to some of the reasons why the superceded systems failed. In chapter three an overview of the relational database is given. Chapter four contains a description of the database in great detail, with a field-by-field explanation of the purposes each field serves. Finally, in chapter five I relate some avenues that I am currently considering for the enhancement of the current system to make it even more easy to use for the Archives staff and more accessible to the Archives public users. In many ways I see the database, and this report, as a starting point, rather than an end.

Acknowledgments

In the course of developing the database, and in the course of writing this report, I have had a great deal of assistance. I would like to give special thanks to the following people: Gary Gisondi, for his guidance and instruction in the mysterious ways of *Advanced Revelation;* Don McCormick, Christine Hoffmann, Adrian Cosentini, Seth Winner, and all the rest of the staff at R&H for their patience, advice, and feedback while this system was created in their midst; and Richard Smiraglia for goading me into writing this report. And finally, I'd like to thank Julius.

Chapter 1: Background

• Introduction • Bibliographic Control versus Archival Control • Sound Recordings as a Special Case • Reconciling Item-Level Cataloging with Archival Group Processing • Describing Archival Sound Recordings • Data Formats for Archival Sound Recordings Collections • Conclusion

Introduction

Historically, the two information fields of libraries and archives have been regarded, and have regarded themselves, as separate disciplines working with distinctly different types of material.[1] In recent years, however, the two fields have begun to share information and practices, as each profession has become increasingly aware of the similarities between them. A catalyst for this is the desire to achieve universal access to knowledge, regardless of the format or type of material that might contain that knowledge.

One area in which the lines of distinction between archival and library practices have begun to converge is that of description and access to sound recordings. That sound recordings could even be described in archival terms was still open to debate when *Archives, Personal Papers, and Manuscripts (APPM)* was first published in 1983.[2] More recent literature, including the second edition of *APPM*, has demonstrated that sound recordings can be archival and should be described following archival practices where necessary.[3] But while there has been some discussion about the need to follow archival descriptive practices for sound recordings, there has been little discussion about the methods by which this sort of description can be achieved. This report was written to discuss the methods and logic behind a specific database application that was created to meet the special needs of a sound recordings repository and its users.

Bibliographic Control versus Archival Control

In order to understand the special needs of a sound recordings repository, it is important to understand the differences between descriptive practices for sound recordings when using bibliographic control as opposed to archival control, and how these differences affect both what is normally found in descriptive records and what the user expects to find in them. Bibliographic and archival descriptive methods are different in large part because the types of material being described are different.[4] Libraries collect materials (commerically-produced monographs, serials, etc.) that are consciously created and planned to be used as units; they are for the most part made for public consumption. Because of this, the unit of description is well-defined. A book contains a work that is complete in and of itself, which is deliberately created by a person or persons. Archival material, on the other hand, is not created or planned as a unit, but rather results from gathering and assembling by some person or group carrying out an activity. The unit of description is less concrete. A collection of correspondence, for example, might consist of an unspecified number of items that are taken as a whole because of their common origin, not because they were intended by anyone to be considered as a group. The difference in the nature of the material being described has resulted in two descriptive practices that have very different emphases.

Bibliographic description is usually based on the concept that a single bibliographic record represents a single publication in a library's collection.[5] A bibliographic record is based on the unit of publication and assumes that an issued publication is complete in and of itself. A bibliographic record contains a description of a specific publication, and includes enough information so that the library user can locate and distinguish different bibliographic items. This bibliographic record also contains access points that allow the user to locate additional works within that bibliographic record.

Thus, a library's catalog is primarily a representation of single publications in the library.

Archival description, however, cannot rely on the unit of publication to provide the focus for description, since archival materials usually are not published. Instead, archival control uses provenance as the descriptive focus, under the assumption that materials with a common origin gain research value through their association with one another. An archival collection record outlines a collection's overall content, while directing users to a secondary description of a collection, the finding aid, to provide direct access to works within the collection. The finding aid then becomes a major point of access for an archival collection, while the catalog record serves mainly to give the researcher broader access.

These two approaches to describing materials are in many ways opposed to one another. Bibliographic description attempts to separate information to allow exact access to the material being described, while archival control strives to give a broader access to the material. Archival description aims to give the researcher a larger view of a range of information, while bibliographic description attempts to provide a detailed view of information. Library materials are important for their informational value, while archival materials are often most important for their contextual value. In other words, library materials present the user with information directly, while the user of archival material often must derive meaning from the aggregate.

Sound Recordings as a Special Case

The contrary approaches to description are exaggerated when sound recordings are considered. This is true because the clientele of libraries have come to expect access at an even greater level of detail than library users of textual material. One major factor in sound recordings description is that different *performances* of any given work must be tracked. This adds an additional dimension that greatly increases the amount of information that must be retrievable. In addition to tracking a work and the names of the creators associated with that work, sound recordings description must also identify and distinguish the different performances and performers of that work. A second major factor in sound recordings description is the fact that sound recordings frequently contain multiple works on single *discographic items*,[6] each of which must be accessible to library users. These needs dictate that sound recordings bibliographic description usually has more detailed information than even textual-material bibliographic description, which itself generally has greater detail than archival description. Thus the difference in the detail of description found in bibliographic and archival cataloging of sound recordings material is even greater than it is for textual material.

Reconciling Item-Level Cataloging with Archival Group Processing

While both archival description and bibliographic description aim to provide researchers with descriptive information about the materials that an institution owns, the two methods achieve these goals in different, often contrary, ways. Library descriptive practice focuses on the bibliographic item, largely ignoring an item's contextual value, since each item was purposefully created to exist separately. Archival description emphasizes this contextual information in order to bring out the relationships among items. Library descriptive practice results in item-level catalog records, while archival descriptive practice results in collection- or series-level finding aids.

A system that provides access to materials in both library and archival manners somehow must resolve these conflicting methods of description. Some method must be found to reconcile the need for content access to data with the need for contextual access to the same data. For archival sound recordings this problem is exacerbated, since sound recordings include the additional layer of information describing performances contained in a recording or collection of recordings.

Intellectually, archival sound recordings for the most part can be treated following standard archival practices, since the definition of what constitutes an archival entity need not be format-specific.[7] However, in order to serve both library and archival users, there are a number of aspects of sound recordings that will affect how archivists describe them.

One important aspect of archival sound recordings is that they still contain individual works to which many users will want to have access, such as the individual pieces of music in a concert. Researchers using sound recordings in libraries have come to expect direct access to data at this level, since it has been provided in discographic description for some time; they need to be able to track down these individual works. This level of detail must be retained in indexes to archival sound recordings—in addition to series-level contextual data, which must be tracked in order to provide important archival information about these materials. The description of archival sound recordings collections, therefore, will contain a much higher level of detail in finding aids than is usual in finding aids for textual archival material.

This high level of detail also is needed for archival research. Archival users need to be able to browse through material on a larger scale, in order to discern the context of any given item. This need for browsing capability is severely hampered by the physical limitations imposed by sound recordings. Due to their size, their fragility, and the need for special equipment for audition, sound recordings collections usually cannot be browsed. While users of textual archival collections can sift through hundreds of items in a collection at a time, users of archival sound recordings collections would be forced to listen to each recording—a time-consuming process, even if it could be done without damaging the material. Thus, even for archival use, this level of detail must be included.

The emphasis on analytic information in finding aids for archival sound recordings collections dictates that these finding aids will be much more involved and lengthy than finding aids for archival collections of textual materials. However, this attention to detail can lead to a loss of contextual information—the description can "lose the forest for the trees," so to speak. For example, a collection of field recordings might have several hundred samples of different ethnic music types, each of which might be important to a given user. However, the collection originally may have been organized by continent, which could give another user a different—yet still important—means of access. If the collection is described individually, the second user might miss contextual information, while if it is described by continent, the first user might miss content information. A method must be found, if possible, to provide the different users of archival sound recordings collections access on both the contextual and the content levels.

Describing Archival Sound Recordings

The discussion above covers some of the general differences between bibliographic and archival control, but not the specific types of data that need to be provided in a system that gives information about archival sound recordings collections on both planes. Soergel has pointed out: "the best way to design or understand a data base is to consider the topics for which the data base is to be

searched."[8] However, without a clearer sense of the use that the
materials currently receive and the use they might receive in the
future, this sort of detailed analysis cannot be attempted; furthermore, attempting to analyze all the data types that might be necessary in an ideal archival information system is beyond the scope of
this report. Rather, the archival sound recordings database grew
from the desire to provide access to recordings in ways that library
and archives user groups currently expect and receive from current
bibliographic sources.

> Archival description presents information about:
>> the provenance of a collection,
>> the creators of a collection,
>> the types of material contained in a collection,
>> and the subjects it covers.
> Bibliographic description presents information about:
>> the author of a work,
>> specific editions of a work,
>> and the subjects of a work.

An information system that provides both the archival and
the library user with important information about archival sound
recordings collections must keep track of data in a number of ways,
which have been organized here into five levels. These levels are:

1. *The collection level*, which allows researchers to identify the
provenance and overall extent of a collection. For example, a
collection might contain recordings of a symphony orchestra, or
it might contain the proceedings of an organization's annual
conferences.

2. *The series level*, which organizes a collection into large
groups according to form of content or original function. For
example, the orchestral collection might be divided into performance and rehearsal series, or the annual conferences might be
subdivided by committee or year.

3. *The discographic-item level*, which provides the user with information concerning single discographic entities in a collection. Examples of discographic items would be a recording of a single concert of the orchestra or a particular panel discussion at a conference.

4. *The work level*, which identifies specific works within a discographic item. Examples of works would be Brahms' *First Symphony* performed as part of a concert or a speech given as part of the panel discussion.

5. *The physical-item level*, which identifies actual physical items within a collection. Examples would be the 12-inch 78 rpm acetate disc that contains sides 5 and 7 of the radio concert (the set might have 8 discs and 16 sides) containing parts 1 and 3 of Brahms' *First Symphony*, or the third cassette of the panel discussion, which contains the first part of a speech.

While these levels can be identified and tracked in textual archival collections, in many cases it has been considered unnecessary because archival users generally are not seen as needing this sort of detailed information. Most textual archival material is described only at the collection, series, and the bibliographic (i.e. discographic) levels, since archives can rely on the end-user being able to browse through portions of a collection. Because of this capability, archival description at the individual work- or physical item-level is more the exception than the rule. For archival sound recordings, however, this sort of detail is critical.

Data Formats for Archival Sound Recordings Collections

Each of the levels described above represents a different entity within the descriptive realm of archival sound recordings collections.[9] Keeping track of data on these multiple levels can become quite complicated, especially because the levels frequently overlap. For example, a performance of a Brahms symphony (a work) might be part of a radio concert (a discographic item), but be recorded on three sides of three acetate discs (physical items).

A linear descriptive method, one in which a single definition of a unit is used, will result in compromises in the accuracy, retrievability, or value of the information retrieved. For example, using the physical item as the unit of description in the instance given above will result in three listings for the Brahms symphony (one for each disc on which the symphony is recorded), and at least three (and possibly many more) listings for the radio concert (one for each disc of the symphony, plus one for each of the remaining discs in the concert). If either the work or the concert is used to define the unit, other types of information are lost.

Instead, a relational structure can be used much more efficiently. In this sort of structure, each entity is described separately and links among the entities are made to delineate the interrelationships. By separating entities, only those aspects that pertain to a given entity must be identified within that entity description, which eliminates ambiguous or redundant data. Once each entity is fully described, links between the entities can be made to register more complex data about a given entity. Thus, with the Brahms symphony performance mentioned before, a number of different unit descriptions would be made: one for the collection, one for the radio concert, one for the symphony, and one each for the discs that contain the concert. Each record would only have to identify information pertinent to the unit being described; subsequently, appropriate links would be made.

This multi-level approach, wherein each type of entity is described in the same manner as other entities of its type, but differently from other entity types, is the approach that the archival sound recordings database uses. While it was not possible for all of the pertinent or important entities and relationships to be identified and separated, the application does at least identify some of the more prominent ones.

Conclusion

The Rodgers & Hammerstein Archives of Recorded Sound (R&H), despite its sound recordings focus, found that many of its noncommercial recordings had contextual information that needed to be documented, and that processing these sound recordings using archival descriptive practices would bring out this information. However, the needs of R&H's users dictated that the analytic detail contained in standard discographic descriptions had to be included for archival sound recordings as well. An information system that provides both the archival and library user with important information about archival sound recordings collections must accommodate at least five levels of data: collection, series, discographic item, work, and physical item.

A number of different methods of data capture were tried and rejected at R&H. Eventually a relational database was designed to meet the sometimes conflicting needs of archival and library users of archival sound recordings collections. In chapter 2 the process by which we came to use a relational database is described. The remainder of this report, chapters 3–5, describes that database.

References and Notes

1. Richard P. Smiraglia, "New Promise for the Universal Control of Recorded Knowledge," *Cataloging and Classification Quarterly*, 11, no. 3/4 (1990): 2–3.

2. "Such non-textual materials as graphics (including photographs), machine-readable files, and motion pictures and videorecordings may be cataloged according to other rules." Steven L. Hensen, *Archives, Personal Papers, and Manuscripts: a Cataloging Manual for Archival Repositories, Historical Societies, and Manuscript Libraries* (Washington, D.C.: Library of Congress, 1983), p. 8.

3. See for instance, Steven L. Hensen, *Archives, Personal Papers, and Manuscripts: a Cataloging Manual for Archival Repositories, Historical Societies, and Manuscript Libraries*, 2d ed. (Chicago: Society of American Archivists, 1989), p. 4–5; David H. Thomas, "Cataloging Sound Recordings Using Archival Methods" *Cataloging and Classification Quarterly* 11, no. 3/4 (1990): 193–212; and, Alan Ward, *A Manual of Sound Archive Administration* (Aldershot, Hauts; Brookfield, Vt.: Gower, 1990).

4. Michael J. Fox. "Descriptive Cataloging for Archival Materials," *Cataloging and Classification Quarterly* 11, no. 3/4 (1990): 17.

5. While "In" analytics are an option for providing highly-detailed access to complex bibliographic entities (cf. *Anglo-American Cataloguing Rules*, 2d ed., 1988 revision, Chapter 13), this method of description is not commonly used for sound recordings.

6. A discographic item is the sound recording equivalent of a bibliographic item. The word "bibliographic" implies a textual document, whereas this report discusses only sound recordings. Therefore the word "discographic" will be used instead of "bibliographic" where applicable. (The term "audiographic," while technically more accurate still than "discographic," is not in common use, and will not be used here.)

7. See especially Thomas, "Cataloging Sound Recordings."

8. Dagobert Soergel, *Organizing Information : Principles of Data Base and Retrieval Systems* (Orlando, FL: Harcourt, 1985), p. 21.

9. See Soergel, *Organizing Information*, for more on relational data structures.

Chapter 2: The Archives and the Evolution of the Application

• Introduction • The Archives: Background and History • The Noncommercial Sound Recordings Project • Evolution of an Application • A Work-Based Descriptive System • An Item-Based Descriptive System • An Event-Based Descriptive System, With Standard (Nonrelational) Data Format • The Basis of the Nonrelational Data Structure • An Event-Based Descriptive System, With Relational Structure • Conclusion

Introduction

An information system is developed to meet the specific or perceived needs of a user or group of users whose needs can be vastly different and sometimes in conflict. In order to develop such an application, therefore, it is necessary to identify the users and their needs and to strive to accommodate them. Both users and needs can be local or national; an application will strive to meet all needs. In this chapter the reader is presented a brief history of the Archives for which the archival sound recordings database was developed and a description of the process of attempting to meet the needs of both the Archives and its users.

The Archives: Background and History

The Rodgers and Hammerstein Archives of Recorded Sound (R&H) is the primary sound recordings research collection for The New York Public Library. As such, R&H has holdings that cover wide subject areas, including Western art music, popular and folk music from around the world, jazz, radio broadcast material, and spoken word recordings. These holdings serve a wide range of researchers: actors wishing to learn accents, operatic singers wishing to study for a specific role, discographers, broadcasters and film makers doing background research, among others.

The Archives contains approximately 500,000 sound recordings in all formats—discs in a wide variety of sizes and speeds, reel to reel tapes in all sizes and widths, cassettes, videotapes, wire recordings, cylinders, and compact discs. The majority of the materials in the collection are commercial recordings—that is, recordings produced by some company with the aim of selling these recordings to an indeterminate paying audience. However, some thirty thousand items are noncommercial recordings—recordings that were made for various reasons on a largely singular basis, for a specific user or group, and not for sale to a buying public.

These noncommercial recordings have been donated by a wide variety of people, including record collectors, radio personalities, authors, composers, and institutions such as radio stations. In many cases, donors are or were important professionals in the field their recordings document, such as the conductor Arturo Toscanini or the radio writing team of Jerome Lawrence and Bob Lee. In many cases, these recordings document the activities of persons or groups as they carried out their profession or business. For example, Toscanini's career as a conductor can be studied from the extensive rehearsal and concert recordings that were made and collected by him. This collection might be used to study his rehearsal techniques or the changes in the performance of a specific work over the course of his career.

The recordings have been collected by the Archives for over twenty years; however, until 1986, very little was done to catalog or preserve these recordings. The major difficulties in describing and processing these materials spring from their unique nature, which requires techniques that are different from those used with commercially-issued materials. Discographically, noncommercial recordings often have little or no documentation concerning their contents, since the owner of the recordings was usually quite familiar with their contents and could identify materials from very brief descriptions. Physically, noncommercial recordings often have obscure formats or use variant recording technologies that are poorly documented and difficult to recreate on modern equipment.

The difficulties of discographic description and physical treatment, combined with limited staffing, meant that little was done to catalog and preserve these special collections. In 1986, however, the Archives sought grant monies to implement preservation and descriptive programs designed specifically to handle these recordings. The grant proposals sought to address the three major technical service needs of the Archives regarding special collection sound recordings: cleaning and rehousing them, describing them, and transferring them to a stable playback medium.

The Noncommercial Sound Recordings Project

The original grant for processing noncommercial sound recordings, which was funded by New York State, supported one archivist and one part time clerk. This grant was succeeded by two one year grants funded by the U.S. Department of Education, which supported three full time archivists and a varying number of clerks. Each of these grants had two major facets to it: the first was to catalog these recordings, and the second was to clean them for future transfer activity. It was proposed that archival control techniques should be used for the descriptive phases of the projects, because in preliminary examinations it was determined that these recordings possessed many of the qualities by which archivists identify archival materials. Archival sound recordings collections would be described following standard guidelines, and MARC-AMC (Ar-

chives and Manuscripts Control) records for these archival entities
would be entered in the Research Libraries Information Network
(RLIN). The aim of the cleaning portion of the projects was to clean
the recordings so they could then be queued for preservation. A related grant funded this preservation process, in which original
sound recordings were copied in real-time on analog reel-to-reel
tapes.

The descriptive needs of archival sound recordings collections dictate that finding aids for these materials will be far more
detail-oriented and complex than finding aids for textual materials.
In order to establish the best mechanical method to handle these
discographic issues, early work on collections primarily addressed
itself to descriptive rather than preservation issues. Methods of description needed to be worked out that would include the large
amount of analytic discographic information in a finding aid clearly
and efficiently, while at the same time maintaining the larger archival structure. The actual methods that were employed are discussed later in this chapter. While these descriptive methods were
being established, the effort to coordinate description and cleaning
with the work of preservation engineers was set aside.

Once the basic descriptive issues were more or less resolved,
the cleaning portion of the project began with the hope that preservation transfers could be made quickly. Noncommercial sound recordings historically have been produced on highly unstable materials, and the first step to preserving them is to clean and rehouse
them. It was assumed that by cleaning the recordings while they
were being identified, the transfer process could be expedited. Since
the recordings had to be handled in order to identify and describe
them, it seemed logical to clean and rehouse them at that time. In
practice, it was found that cleaning recordings at the time of the
descriptive process was ill-advised, because the preservation process
often lagged far behind the cleaning process, and the cleaning process often promoted further deterioration. Because of this, it was

deemed better simply to note the condition of recordings for future reference.

Thus the main functions of the project became to catalog the collections and gain intellectual control over the material, and to identify the condition of the materials for future preservation action, while the cleaning and transfer processes were set aside until they could be carried out together.

Evolution of an Application

As mentioned above, guidelines for the descriptive content of archival sound recordings finding aids had to be developed. The Archives decided early on that these finding aids had to contain the fullest information available in order to allow researchers direct access to all individual works in a collection. This was deemed necessary because of the needs of researchers, and the physical limitations both at the Archives (which has closed stacks) and of noncommercial sound recordings in general. The format in which these data were conveyed to the researcher, however, underwent a series of changes.

A WORK-BASED DESCRIPTIVE SYSTEM

The first descriptive methods that were tried to provide this access in a finding aid all used the work as the fundamental unit of description. This approach approximates the use of "In" analytics as suggested by the *Anglo-American Cataloguing Rules*, 2d edition (*AACR2*)[1] in chapter 13. Each entry in a finding aid described an individual work, and noted the fact that the work was performed on a given date by certain performers, which served to link it with the other works on a discographic item. Thus a radio concert of symphonic music was described as several separate entries, because each musical piece within the concert was a work. There was, however, no explicit linking of the works on a concert to a central description of the concert as a whole.

The first finding aids that were created used this descriptive approach. Each entry described a work, and referred the user to the classmarked item(s) containing the work. It would identify the event of which it was a part, such as the radio program on which a work was performed. Work entries would in turn be arranged into discographic and then series order—in this case, first by individual program and then by program title. This would give the researcher a work's context in the collection. A typical entry would list the date, composer, title, performer and classmarks for each work in a broadcast concert, with the radio program being the heading for the list (see figure 2–1).

These finding aids were created using a word processor,[2] but included no indexes because in the word-processing environment there was little recourse for providing access under the other headings associated with a work short of re-keying the entire entry.[3] For example, a name-title heading such as:

Debussy, Claude.
    La mer.

could not readily be changed into the title-name heading:

La mer.
Debussy, Claude.

This greatly limited the flexibility and indexing capability of the finding aid.

This descriptive method captured extensive information about the individual works within a collection, and gave this information in context, but it did not provide direct access to those works. For example, a user could not look in one place to find all of the different performances of Debussy's *La Mer* in a collection,

Figure 2–1: Work-Based Finding Aid Structure

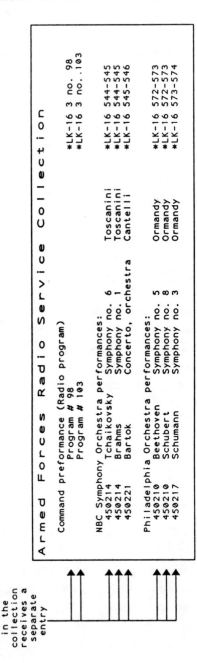

because there were no cumulative indexes. In addition, there was a great loss of the overview of a collection; although the individual works were placed in their appropriate context, the higher levels of organization were not exceedingly clear in the finding aid. Furthermore, there was no way to track the physical characteristics of the materials beyond their basic format (which is the basis of our classmark system), or to identify any treatments that may have been given to these items.

AN ITEM-BASED DESCRIPTIVE SYSTEM

The next descriptive method used was one in which the physical item formed the basis of description. This approach allowed for more accurate identification of physical-item data, such as individual physical characteristics and preservation activity. It was also at this point that a database management program first was used to capture this information in a fielded format, which allowed for more exhaustive indexing.

In using the physical item descriptive method, the first database designs were based on the preservation copy items for a given collection. The basic unit of description was the preservation item, and original items were described within this preservation item record (see figure 2–2). The reasons this approach was taken were purely practical:

1. The first collections that were processed were being preserved—a process that entailed transferring recordings from their original format to a more stable one (usually reel-to-reel tape);
2. The tape copies for these collections identified clearly what works the original items contained, whereas the original often did not; and,
3. By describing the preservation tapes, it was possible to generate tape box labels that identified the contents of each tape clearly.

Figure 2–2: Item-Based Database Structure

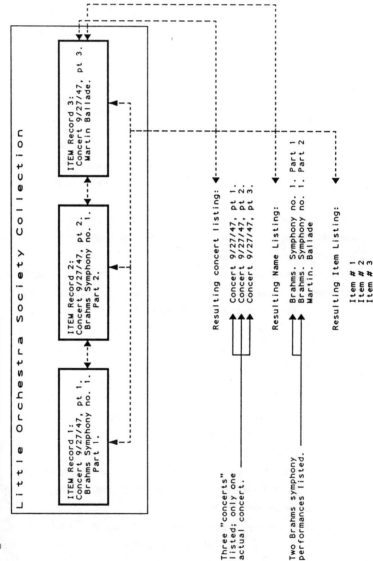

Little Orchestra Society Collection

ITEM Record 1:
Concert 9/27/47, pt 1.
Brahms Symphony no. 1.
Part 1.

ITEM Record 2:
Concert 9/27/47, pt 2.
Brahms Symphony no. 1.
Part 2.

ITEM Record 3:
Concert 9/27/47, pt 3.
Martin Ballade.

Resulting concert listing:

Concert 9/27/47, pt 1.
Concert 9/27/47, pt 2.
Concert 9/27/47, pt 3.

Three "concerts"
listed; only one
actual concert.

Resulting Name Listing:

Brahms. Symphony no. 1. Part 1
Brahms. Symphony no. 1. Part 2
Martin. Ballade

Two Brahms symphony
performances listed.

Resulting Item Listing:

Item # 1
Item # 2
Item # 3

This approach worked well for tracking preservation tapes. Information about the transfer process was captured and maintained, as was information about the various physical items involved. The database program allowed analytic information to be reformatted for finding aids. However, this approach had a number of shortcomings. First, for collections that hadn't been transferred or collections that had only been partly transferred, it was impossible to describe those materials that had not yet been transferred, since the database was structured on the transfer item. Second, it did not cope well with analytic entries for works that spanned more than one preservation tape. Since each tape had to receive a database record, the indexes would contain two references to the single work, one for each part of the work.

Another problem with these early databases was that their field structures were designed on a collection-by-collection basis. While this allowed the archivist the freedom to capture only those data that were pertinent in a given collection, it resulted in a number of problems. It took a great deal of the archivist's time to develop these unique database structures, and they required time for project staff to learn. Each finding aid had to be formatted individually by the archivist, which slowed down processing. Using different data structures also confounded any attempts to use the data in an on- line environment, since the data were not in a single format, and thus could not be searched or formatted reliably.

AN EVENT-BASED DESCRIPTIVE SYSTEM, WITH STANDARD (NONRELATIONAL) DATA FORMAT

A standard descriptive system then was adopted that was based on the idea of a "recorded event" as the focal point of description, with description of individual works included in this "event" (see figure 2–3). A recorded event defined loosely as any recording that was created *intentionally* to exist as a unit. As such, a

Figure 2–3: Event-Based Database Structure (Nonrelational)

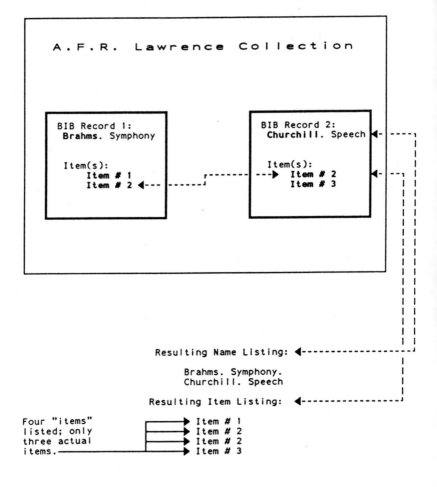

recorded event could contain either individual or multiple works.
An event could thus comprise one musical work, a radio broadcast
concert of popular music, a tape reel of political speeches recorded
at various times on a particular topic, or a test pressing of songs for
potential release. This definition roughly corresponds to the defini-

tion of a published discographic unit, although it is a little less concrete.

The emphasis on intentional creation is important. Archival collections are primarily unpublished material; as such, there is no unifying publication element. For sound recordings, a single physical item might contain widely disparate recordings simply because there was extra room on the item. Describing the two works together because they are on one physical unit probably will result in a strange description that does not clearly inform users of the nature of the material, which will not serve users' needs. While it is of course practically impossible to determine the intent behind what has been put on a given recording, it is nonetheless necessary with archival sound recordings to attempt to make this distinction.

An example of two separate events occurring on overlapping items is a set of discs that contain a recording of Brahms' *Requiem* on three sides of the two discs and a speech given by Winston Churchill on the fourth side. The *Requiem* was recorded from the radio station WJZ on April 11, 1941. The Churchill speech also was recorded from WJZ, but on September 11, 1940. These two events apparently have nothing to do with each other, except that the person doing the recording efficiently made use of an available blank side to record something else of interest. There is no apparent link between the events on these two discs; their subject content, recording dates and sources all differ.

The Basis of the Nonrelational Data Structure

The standardized data structure that was adopted for this nonrelational database was derived from the MARC format for sound recordings, and contained fields analogous to fields 007, 245, 500, 505, 700, 710, and 740. Although the actual format and order of these fields differed from MARC, the data content for these fields was essentially the same; thus the data could be made MARC-compatible. The record structure included fields for format and condition information of individual physical items to be noted separately within the discographic record, and fields for tracking preservation items were included. Provenance was maintained by giving each archival collection a separate data file in the database environment.

This database structure, although based on MARC, departed significantly from it in a number of areas. One major departure was in the formatted contents note area (MARC 505), which was omitted from this database. In MARC, field 505 contains contents transcribed from the item; indexing for works listed in the 505 must be entered separately. Because the Archives knew in advance that it wanted full analytic access to contents notes, separate fields were created for the title, composer and duration data that make up a contents note. This allowed each element to be indexed separately, while the program's formatting functions could then take these data and reconfigure them into a formatted 505 note as needed.

Another major departure from MARC was in the extent of item area (MARC 300). The data content in the MARC 300 field is largely duplicated in the 007 fixed field area. We found that the 007 data could be used to create the physical description programmatically and omit the MARC 300 field from the local record altogether, thus eliminating typing errors and the need to know the appropriate format of the extent of item area. While the one-letter codes of the 007 were difficult to remember, field by field pop-ups provided help to the inputter.

Using separate data files to track provenance was similar to the methods used in earlier databases, except that each file now had the same data structure. Standardizing the database gave it a number of advantages over earlier ones. Development of database structures and data entry windows was eliminated, since each collection could use already established formats. Input procedures were streamlined so that any staff member could work on any collection with a minimum of time needed to learn a new database. Since collections processed using this database all had the same data structure, the task of formatting output for reports could be streamlined, and the process of creating a finding aid could be automated.

However, in using this database, two major shortcomings were observed. The first shortcoming was that the ability to identify the exact location of a work within a discographic entity on the physical item was lost if there was more than one physical item. In the physical-item-based database, it was possible to state clearly where a work was located on a given item. For example, if a specific work was the third work on a disc, it would appear in the contents as the third work. However, in the discographic-item-based database, this disc might be the second in a three record set, thus making this work the seventh listed in a contents note. Because there was only one area that contained the contents data for all the items, there was no way to point directly to a work's location on a single item, since there was more than one item included in the record. This lack of specificity became even more acutely obvious when a preservation copy had been made, and there were two full copies for each work.

Second, this approach forced compromises when multiple works were stored on overlapping physical items. In this database structure, the Brahms symphony and the Churchill speech discussed above could not be described accurately. The archivist had to choose between describing these two discographic items together or separately, because the database incorporated the item descriptions as part of the discographic record. Describing the two recordings together as a set implies that the two events somehow belong together when in fact they may not have been created for any specific purpose other than convenience. Furthermore, because the set has no identifying title and no clear overall description, the cataloger had to create a title that describes the two disparate items as one—in the example above, the cataloger chose the heading "Music and Churchill speech." Describing the two entities separately, however, results in two separate physical descriptions, both of which incorrectly identify the extent of the recording, with an extra disc "appearing" because of the overlap (again, see figure 2–3).

AN EVENT-BASED DESCRIPTIVE SYSTEM, WITH RELATIONAL STRUCTURE

It became clear that to address these shortcomings while at the same time retaining the functionality of the current design, the database needed to be restructured radically. To assist in inventory control, the ideal database would allow physical-item-level data to be tracked independently of the discographic information, while maintaining the inherent link between the discographic and physical descriptions. For archival researchers, it would maintain the contextual structure of the collection, while it would allow those researchers who needed specific works by specific performers to find that information. To serve the needs of the transfer engineers, it would allow discographic and physical data already entered into the database to be reused to identify materials for transfer, and require engineers only to add transfer data to the database. Finally, it would allow for integration into an online environment, with the potential to search all the Archives' holdings at once.

Each of these goals easily can be attained separately, and in fact already had been attained at some point in earlier databases at the Archives. However, creating a database that accomplished all these goals simultaneously was more difficult, and was complicated by the fact that these goals often are at odds with one another. For example, maintaining collection-level integrity had been accomplished by using separate data files—at the cost of online searching capabilities. Keeping track of the contents of individual physical items could be done by using the physical item as the basis of de scription—if the multiple headings that resulted could be accepted in a finding aid and online.

The relational database that was proposed to address all these needs was one in which collection-level data would be stored in a collection file, discographic data would be stored in another file, and physical item data would be stored in a third file (see figure 2–4). Links would be maintained between the levels to identify which records in each data file belong to one another. These links would be reciprocal, so that, for example, the collection ID would be stored in each discographic item record while the discographic ID would be stored in a collection list.

This segmented structure solves the problems that earlier databases presented in choosing between describing the physical or the discographic item. By separating the contextual, discographic, and physical levels of control, it theoretically becomes possible to describe the A.F.R. Lawrence collection in a single archival record, to describe the Brahms *Requiem* and the Churchill speech in separate discographic records, to describe the physical items that make up these discographic entities in separate physical item records, and finally to perform the appropriate links among the collection, discographic and physical levels. This basic structure addresses most of the needs listed above: accurate inventory control can be maintained, redundant headings can be eliminated, and online searching can be done. With a little more enhancement, it becomes possible to add cross-referencing within the item data file to allow transfer information to be maintained (see figure 2–5), thus satisfying the transfer engineer's needs as well.

A relational database program easily accommodates the linking of records in one file to records in another, so that setting up a database that links many physical items to one discographic record, and many discographic records to one collection record can be reasonably straightforward. By working from the largest to the

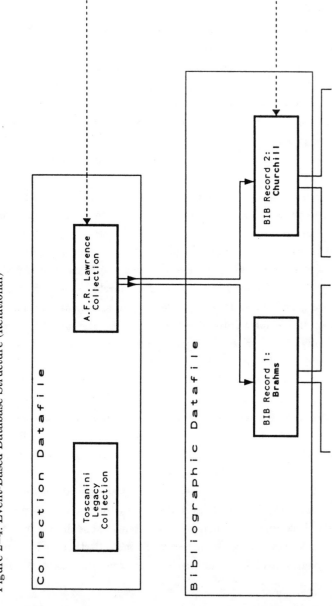

Figure 2–4: Event-Based Database Structure (Relational)

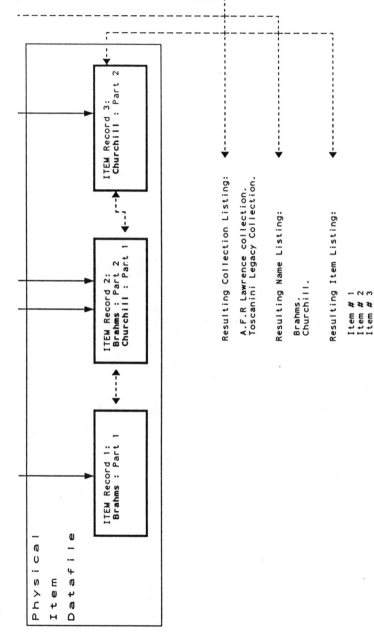

Figure 2–4: *(continued)*

Figure 2–5: Transfer Information

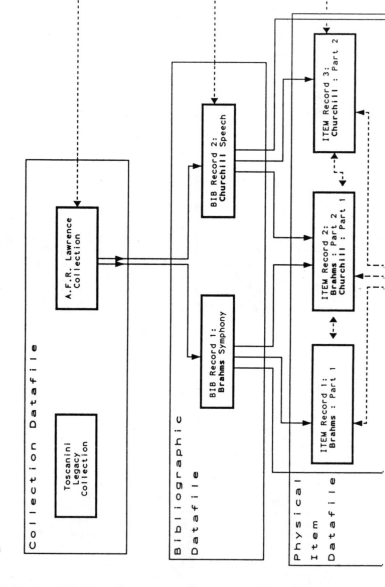

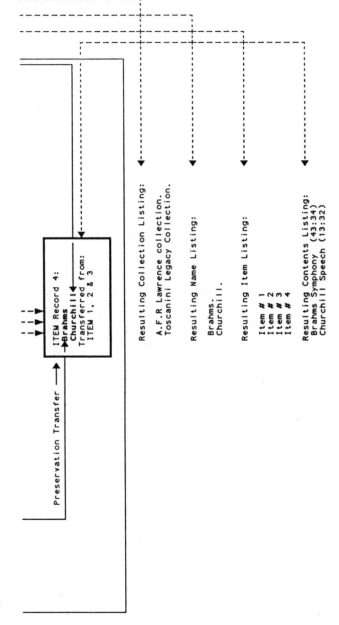

Figure 2-5 *(continued)*

Preservation Transfer

ITEM Record 4:
Brahms
Churchill
Transferred from:
ITEM 1, 2 & 3

Resulting Collection Listing:

A.F.R Lawrence collection.
Toscanini Legacy Collection.

Resulting Name Listing:

Brahms.
Churchill.

Resulting Item Listing:

Item # 1
Item # 2
Item # 3
Item # 4

Resulting Contents Listing:
Brahms Symphony (43:34)
Churchill Speech (13:32)

smallest unit of description, a pyramid structure can be created. Each smaller unit in the chain automatically stores a pointer to the next level up (see figure 2–6). Thus the relationships between the A.F.R. Lawrence collection and the Brahms requiem, between the requiem and the two discs that contain it, and between the requiem and the Churchill speech clearly can be identified.

However, linking from the bottom of the pyramid upward to the top—a feature that had to be available in this database, in order to allow one physical item to be linked to more than one discographic item—can be much more complicated. While placing pointers from the top down can be done automatically, pointers from the bottom up must be placed in the record manually. Because the standard input procedure moves from the top of the hierarchy to the bottom, it is possible to place the ID for the higher unit in the lower one automatically (again, see figure 2–6).

However, there is no automatic method by which the system can retrieve an ID from a higher level; this must be done explicitly by the user (see figure 2–7). First, the user must be allowed to choose which discographic records need to be linked to the current physical item (see figure 2–7, step 1). The user must be able to make this choice from a listing of extant discographic records. The system then must verify that the record actually exists, and that the selected record isn't already linked to the current physical record (see figure 2–7, Step 2). The system must allow the inputter to specify the order in which the discographic records occur on the physical item, so that future users can locate specific materials rapidly (see figure 2–7, Step 3). And the system must allow the user to derive physical-item contents from the multiple discographic records linked to the current physical item.

Once the issue of maintaining links across files had been solved, most procedures had to be reconsidered in view of the new structure. For example, displaying all items in a collection was relatively simple in earlier systems—the user merely listed an entire

Figure 2–6: Pointer Maintenance

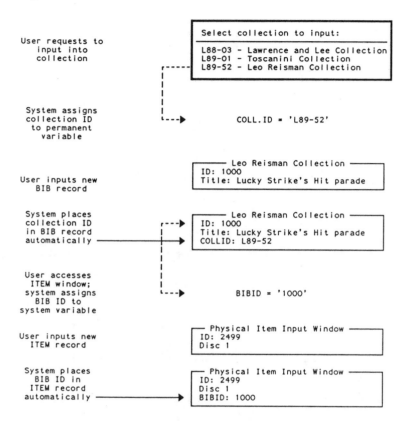

data file. In the new system, the global discographic data file must
first be pre-processed to eliminate all records from other collections.
A second example is the program to create the physical description.
In earlier database structures, the program had only to extract
physical description data from the currently active record, whereas
with the new structure the data had to be gathered from separate
physical-item records. Each of the processes that the database had
provided previously had to be accommodated in the new database
without rendering other functions impossible.

Figure 2–7: Pointer Installation from Bottom Up

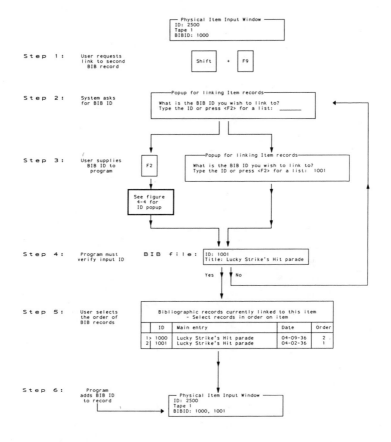

Conclusion

The descriptive needs of archival sound recordings collections dictate that finding aids for these materials will be far more detail-oriented and complex than finding aids for textual materials. A variety of solutions, ranging from word-processed finding aids to individually designed databases were tried and rejected at R&H. Finally a relational database structure was implemented. In chapter 3, an overview of the relational structure is presented. This is followed, in chapter 4, by a field-by-field description of the database.

References and Notes

1. *Anglo-American Cataloguing Rules*, 2d ed., 1988 revision (Chicago: American Library Association, 1988).

2. The word processing program used for these finding aids was *Nota Bene* versions 2 and 3. In order to differentiate between elements in the list, *Nota Bene*'s "cellular tabs" feature was used.

3. Key macros were developed that took the elements in the *Nota Bene* cellular tab format and rearranged them in different orders. These macros, however, were extremely slow.

Chapter 3: Overview of the Database

Introduction

In preceding chapters we learned that archival information systems for sound recordings need to provide data at varying levels of detail to both users and staff. Furthermore, archival information systems need to be dynamic. That is, in the course of preserving and processing archival materials, it is necessary continually to edit and update descriptive data. A relational database program easily accommodates the linking of records in one file to records in another, making it possible to link many physical items to one discographic record, and many discographic records to one collection record. At R&H we discovered that an event-based descriptive system with relational structure would meet all of these requirements.

This chapter gives an overview of the database that was designed to process noncommercial sound recordings. The noncommercial archival sound recordings database utilizes collection, discographic-, and physical-item data files to meet a variety of functions. Those files and the functions they serve are described below.

Goals of the Application

The archival sound recordings database aims to meet a number of different goals. It was created to serve the immediate needs of a specific project. Furthermore, it was created in response to shortcomings observed in earlier database formats. Its first goal was to simplify the description of archival sound recordings, so that finding aids could be produced quickly and efficiently. Because of the Archives' stated access policies, the descriptions that the database created had to provide detailed content access to material comparable to traditional discographic description—including analytic access to individual works and performers, as well as direct references to individual physical items—in addition to providing users with contextual access to larger archival units. In order to do this, the database had to maintain information on at least five levels —collection, series, discographic, work, and physical levels—which are maintained in three data files, with relational links among them.

A second goal of the database was to bring all technical processing of these materials under one program, which includes tracking *condition states* of individual physical items, *preservation treatments* carried out on these items, and *transfer information*, as well as *shelflisting capabilities*. Because of the wide variation in format and recording characteristics of archival recordings, the system had to provide storage of this highly detailed and complex information at the physical-item level.

Finally, the database was designed with the hope that on-line public access to this information would be possible. Public users of the database would have to be able to search all the archival holdings in as simple and straightforward a manner as possible. The database had to allow for the possibility, even if it didn't provide this access immediately.

The Software

One major reason for using a database manager to track finding aid information is that most finding aids take one set of data and rearrange it in a number of ways to provide direct access to different aspects of the information. For example, the main portion of a finding aid for a collection of correspondence might describe folders within the collection, and then mention some of the names of writers that occur in each folder. A names index then would list these names alphabetically, and refer the user to the appropriate folder. In a relatively sketchy finding aid, it is possible to create this sort of index in a word-processing program. However, in a highly-detailed archival sound recordings collection finding aid, this becomes increasingly unwieldy as the number of names and works mounts. The repeated use of a single piece of data and the relatively large number of different data types (for example, names, titles, type of recording, classmarks, etc.), combined with the high degree of detail required by archival sound recordings, makes a database manager highly desirable.

Another reason to use a database manager to store finding aid information is that fielded information can be searched online more readily than word processing text files can. Data that are stored in separate fields can be identified and indexed separately thus allowing the end-user more detailed access to those data. Thus a user of a fielded database can search for works with the word "Lincoln" in the title without also retrieving works that were written or performed by persons whose names are "Lincoln." While a number of programs allow users to search text files for any sort of text, these programs cannot make any distinction between types of data, since there is nothing in the original data to differentiate these types. With a database structure, it becomes possible to make these finer distinctions. In addition, structured databases potentially can contain a much larger data set than text searching programs and retrieve records from that data-set much faster than any text-based search engine. This is due to the fact that a database can contain many indexes, each of which covers a different portion of the data in the whole file.

The fielded structure of a database management program allows one set of information that is captured in the database to be manipulated in a great variety of ways. Displays can be restructured, indexes reconfigured, output reformatted—all from the same basic data set, since the pieces of information are discrete. Features can be added to the system without reconstructing the basic data. For example, transfer engineers can print, at a keystroke, cue sheets listing all contents; transfer data for preservation tapes can be printed using the same data that are used to create the finding aid. Storing the basic data in separate fields enables information to be used much more flexibly.

Because of these demonstrated needs, we chose to use a database management program rather than a word processor. The database management software that was chosen for the project was *Advanced Revelation (AREV)*, marketed by Revelation Technologies. The main reasons for using *AREV* are the software's ability to accommodate variable length data with a minimum of wasted disk space, its flexible indexing structure, and its programming flexibility.

FIELD LENGTH

Unlike most database management software, *AREV* does not require the developer to decide on field lengths when designing an application. Rather, *AREV* allows any field in a record to use as much space as is allowed by the limitations of the Intel memory-addressing scheme, which is 64 kilobytes. *AREV* accomplishes this flexibility by using delimiters instead of absolute length to determine fields and records. Furthermore, because it uses this delimiter structure, fields use only the space of data within the actual field, not the full length of the defined field as other programs do.

INDEXING

AREV allows the user an unlimited number of indexes, and provides for both word and phrase indexing. The indexes are extremely fast in response time, due to the system's linear hash filing technique. This filing system also enables *AREV* to return results quickly, regardless of the database size.

PROGRAMMING FLEXIBILITY

AREV uses a modified BASIC programming language that allows the developer to control every aspect of the user's environment from cursor movement on screen to verifying data that have been entered by a user on a field-by-field basis. In addition, *AREV* allows the developer a great deal of opportunity to interrupt the system flow in almost any process. Because of this flexibility, it is possible for the developer to maintain a high degree of control of the data within the system while at the same time giving the user much greater help in the input process.

The Database: An Overview

As discussed above, the archival sound recordings database uses a multifile structure to maintain the different levels of organization present in an archival sound recordings collection. It uses relational links between the files to maintain the archival relationships unambiguously. Users input data into the various files of the database by means of *data entry windows*. The files that are used to store the various data are the *COLLECTION*, the *BIB*, and the *ITEM* data files (see figure 3–1).

The *COLLECTION* data file contains records that describe archival sound recordings at the collection level. Each record in the file describes an archival entity with a brief description, which corresponds roughly to the collection-level MARC-AMC record. An example of a collection would be:

> "The A.F.R. Lawrence collection of historical spoken word, 1900–1970."

Figure 3–1: Archival Database Structure Overview

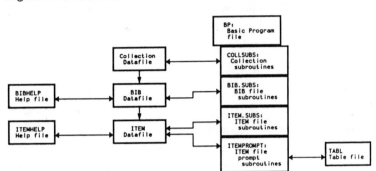

Actions that affect an entire collection, such as creating finding aids and managing workflow, can be carried out in this datafile. The collection record also contains a list of the discographic records that constitute a collection. This list is maintained by the program automatically.

The *BIB* data file contains series-, discographic-, and work-level information. Each record in this file describes a discographic item in an archival entity, whether that item comprises single or multiple works. An example of a discographic item would be:

> "Address to Congress / Franklin D. Roosevelt,
> 12–08–41."

Any discographic record can be assigned to a series by means of the SERIES field. Descriptions of individual works are stored within the discographic-item record, and are indexed individually. Most processing work takes place in this file.

The *ITEM* data file is the one in which each record describes a single physical item. An example of a physical item would be one 78 rpm disc of the four discs that make up the Roosevelt speech mentioned above. In this file all data that describe an actual physical item reside. This includes basic physical characteristics, preservation documentation, and item-level contents information.

The Collection Data File

The first step that must be taken when a collection is processed using the database system is to create a brief collection-level record. This record contains information that for the most part duplicates information in a collection-level MARC-AMC record, and thus may contain as little information as the accession number and the collection name. This provides the system with a focal point around which to organize all further processing in the database. Because these data also are placed in the final collection-level MARC-AMC record, current practice at the Archives is to input very little collection-level data into the local database. In the future, the collection record might be stored only as a MARC record, with fields set aside for local database links.

The main role of the collection record is to gather information about each collection in a single record. Collection name, source of acquisition, and physical extent of the collection are examples of information that the collection record can contain. This corresponds roughly to the role of a collection-level MARC-AMC record. Additionally, the collection data file in the archival database provides the means to process information on the collection level, such as creating finding aids.

The Bibliographic-Item Data File

Once a collection-level record has been created, information for individual discographic items within the collection must be input. The discographic data file (the BIB file) stores this information. Data that are entered in this file supplant the process of creating printed finding aids. The information that would normally be typed into a detailed finding aid is input into this data file where it can be formatted and indexed in a wide variety of ways.

The BIB file data structure loosely follows that of an item cataloged in the MARC recordings or visual materials format, although there are a number of departures. Most importantly, the BIB file lacks the fixed field and physical description data of a MARC record, because that information is maintained in this database in the *ITEM* file. The only explicit references to the physical items are the two items fields, Original Items and New Items; all other information about the physical items (such as format and location information) is stored in the *ITEM* file. These two fields are fields that are calculated and entered by the system when the inputter creates or changes physical-item records, and which the inputter cannot directly change. Other than these two references to the physical material, the BIB file focuses entirely on describing the discographic entity and the works it may contain.

The Physical-Item Data File

The most detailed information about materials in an archival sound recordings collection is stored in the physical item file (the ITEM file). The ITEM file can track the physical characteristics for each item in a collection. Each record in this file represents one physical item, regardless of its intellectual content, with the discographic record acting as the linking element for separate items within a discographic entity. This structure allows the greatest flexibility in description, because minute details of each item can be tracked individually without duplicating discographic information. The system then can take the information from the discrete item records and compile it for use in display and output procedures.

The ITEM file contains a number of fields that correspond roughly to MARC fields; these are fields 007 and 583, which were used largely as defined, and a modified use of field 505. However, there are many fields included in the ITEM record that do not have corollaries in MARC. Most of these fields allow for full documentation of preservation transfer activities, including highly detailed information about specific equipment used to create a preservation copy of an item. For example, the item window will allow transfer engineers to specify the signal processing units used for a certain transfer, and the settings on those pieces of equipment.

Those fields that correspond to the 007 field use codes based on the MARC format 007 field codes for sound recordings, motion pictures, and videorecordings. The database system had to accommodate all of these formats, since an increasing number of the archival collections that R&H receives have film and video material. A brief examination of the MARC definitions for field 007, however, reveals that this field has different structure and content depending on the format of the item being described. For example, Configuration of Playback Channels is placed in 007 byte 4 for sound recordings, and 007 byte 8 for videorecordings and motion pictures. Thus the MARC 007 fields could not simply be adopted without modification, although it was possible for the most part simply to merge the code tables of the different MARC definitions. In some areas, such as those concerning the base and coating materials that make up an item, the MARC 007 fields were not specific enough for the Archives' needs, and locally-developed fields were substituted.

MARC field 583 is defined to track actions taken on a given copy. These actions commonly are preservation actions, and the definition in recent years has been expanded to include the condition state of an item. In order to keep track of item-level condition information in the local database, codes were developed to describe the various condition states and physical treatments of any given item. The condition states were derived from the glossary of terms in the Association of Audio Archives' preservation manual,[1] and from these states, two-letter codes were developed. Similar two-letter codes were created for the treatment procedures that the Archives uses regularly.

In addition to basic physical description information, the item file provides the user with the ability to identify the contents on a specific physical item. This level of detail is important when one is trying to locate a specific work within a discographic entity, since a listing of works on any entity that has several physical items can get no more specific than all of the items in the entity. For example, a recording of Arturo Toscanini and the NBC Symphony Orchestra rehearsing Beethoven's *Ninth Symphony* might be recorded on four reels of tape, with each movement appearing on one reel. In order to allow a researcher to listen only to the portion of the rehearsal that contains the third movement, it must be clearly identified somewhere that reel three is the reel that the researcher needs.

The item file also tracks preservation transfer activity. Adding this function to the database cuts down dramatically on the time needed to document preservation tapes, since it enables transfer engineers to use existing discographic data to describe the contents of preservation transfer. Fields have been provided to document all aspects of the preservation activity, from noting the original source material to the signal processing used to derive the final sound.

Because of the complexity of describing physical items, their contents, and their physical processing, the ITEM file is by far the most complex file in the application. In order to simplify input into this file, all of the technical fields that use codes have help screens and on-line pop-ups that display to the user the valid codes for a given field. These pop-ups are context-sensitive, only displaying to the user currently valid codes as determined by the code in the kind-of-material field. In addition to this help, the system double-checks the input value for a given field against a table of valid values—again based on the kind of material—and will not allow invalid codes to be input.

Special Processes

A number of routines are carried out at each stage of processing to facilitate the various functions that the database provides. These routines use the data that are input and manipulate them to achieve certain goals. These routines are in effect as data are being input and continue until the finding aid is produced. The routines that simplify data input will be described in Chapter 5. Other routines, however, will not be described there; these programs enhance the overall efficiency of the application.

HEADING REVISION

Once data have been input, a separate editing module allows a librarian to sift through all the name and name-title headings in a collection and change variant headings. This module runs as a separate entry window, and includes only those fields that contain headings. From this window, the user can sort a collection by name-title headings (for example, "Berlin, Irving. There's no business like show business."), or by title-name headings (for example, "There's no business like show business. Berlin, Irving."), and view the resulting list. From this list, the user selects those headings to be changed, and the system then brings each record on screen for editing. In this manner, a collection's discographic records can be proofread reasonably quickly.

GENERATING FINDING AIDS

After the data for a collection have been proofread, the finding aid is generated. This process is carried out from the collection entry window from a function key. Upon starting the finding aid program, the user is asked to verify the collection for which a

Figure 3–2: Creating Finding Aids

Before Formatting

After Formatting

Main entry

ASCAP on parade (Radio program), February 1,
1941.{ME}{P}2 sound discs : analog, 78 rpm,
aluminum-based acetate, mono. ; 12 in. {P}{P}Radio
program broadcast over station WMCA, 8:00 pm.{P}On
labels: "A Frankay Recording."{P}Original in: *LJ-12
4094, *LJ-12 4095. {P}Contents: When that man is dead
and gone / Irving Berlin -- A little old church in
England / Irving Berlin.{P}Forms part of: Irving Berlin
Collection. *L(Special) 91-11.

ASCAP on parade (Radio program), February 1, 1941.
2 sound discs : analog, 78 rpm, aluminum-based acetate,
mono. ; 12 in.

Radio program broadcast over station WMCA, 8:00 pm.
On labels: "A Frankay Recording."
Original in: *LJ-12 4094, *LJ-12 4095.
Contents: When that man is dead and gone / Irving Berlin --
A little old church in England / Irving Berlin.
Forms part of: Irving Berlin Collection. *L(Special) 91-11.

Names list

Berlin, Irving. A little old church in England.{C1}
ASCAP on parade (Radio program), February 1, 1941.{C2}
Berlin, Irving. When that man is dead and gone.{C1}
ASCAP on parade (Radio program), February 1, 1941.{C2}

Berlin, Irving. A little old   ASCAP on parade (Radio
   church in England.   program), February 1, 1941.
Berlin, Irving. When that man   ASCAP on parade (Radio
   is dead and gone.   program), February 1, 1941.

Figure 3–2: *(continued)*

Titles list

A little old church in England. Berlin, Irving.{C1}
ASCAP on parade (Radio program), February 1, 1941.{C2}
When that man is dead and gone; Berlin, Irving.{C1}
ASCAP on parade (Radio program), February 1, 1941.{C2}

A little old church in England. Berlin, Irving.
When that man is dead and gone. Berlin, Irving.

ASCAP on parade (Radio program), February 1, 1941.
ASCAP on parade (Radio program), February 1, 1941.

Dates list

February 1, 1941.{C1}ASCAP on parade (Radio program),
February 1, 1941.{C2}

February 1, 1941.

ASCAP on parade (Radio program), February 1, 1941.

finding aid is to be made. Then the user must specify the DOS destination to which the finding aid data will be directed and the basic name that will be used for the destination files.

The system then creates five DOS files for the finding aid data, one each for a main entry listing, a name and name-title index, a title and title-name index, a chronological index, and a subject index. The program takes the data for the collection and reformats them into each layout and exports them to the appropriate DOS file. The data in each of these files are only in a rough layout (see figure 3–2). The Archives uses laser printers to generate its finding aids using proportional fonts, and *AREV* will not format its output properly for those fonts. Therefore, the Archives uses the database report functions to create the rough documents, and a word processor to reformat the data for printing. Within the word processor, this reformatting is done automatically using key macros (see again figure 3–2).

SHELFLISTING

The most recent function added to the database is a program that checks the on-line shelflist for errors or gaps in the database or on the shelves. This program is possible because the Archives uses a format-based shelving and classmarking scheme. Each classmark consists of a format-based prefix and a sequential number. It is possible, then, to sort the item database first by classmark prefix and then by number, and check for gaps in the numbering sequence. The program that does this generates an error report that can then be checked at the shelf to clear up errors in the database or on the shelf. A separate data file has been created to keep track of the gaps that occur for legitimate reasons, such as materials that are processed outside the database, or materials that have been withdrawn; this file then can be checked by the shelflist program when it is run in the future.

Conclusion

The archival sound recordings database utilizes a multifile structure to serve a wide range of needs, from the public user's need for accurate and detailed contents information to the transfer engineer's need to capture minute aspects of the transfer process. The database provides both the flexibility and specificity required to accomplish these goals.

Additional features also support archival functions, such as the program that creates finding aids, the revision window, and the shelflisting capability. In the next chapter, each of these windows is described as they would be encountered by a user working on an archival sound recordings collection.

Reference

1. Association for Recorded Sound Collections, Associated Audio Archives Committee, *Audio Preservation: A Planning Study*, NEH Grant PS-20021–86, 1987.

Chapter 4: Detailed Description of the Database

Introduction

This chapter contains a detailed, field-by-field description of the archival sound recordings database. These fields are described in the order in which they would be encountered by a user working on an archival sound recordings collection. Flowcharts for each aspect of the application can be found in Appendix B, while a listing of the fields and their MARC equivalents is included in Appendix A.

The Collection Data Entry Window

The Collection Data File contains records that describe archival sound recordings at the collection level. The collection data entry window has twelve *real data* fields in it,[1] eleven of which display to the inputter (see figure 4–1). The last field contains a list of related discographic records that describe the given collection, which is maintained automatically by the software. Only three of these fields must be input for the record to be valid: the ID field, the type of record field, and the collection name field. The ID field (ID) contains the unique accession number for the collection, which is assigned when the material arrives at the archives. The record type (TR) field describes the status of a collection in the Archives' processing, because this field is used by subsequent programs to control whether a collection may be processed at the item level. The

Figure 4–1: Collection Data Entry Window

```
┌──────────────────Collection-Level Accession Entry Window──────────────────┐
│                                                                            │
│  ID:                                                   L91.11   Rec.type F │
│  Main.entry:                                                               │
│  Collection.name:        Irving Berlin Collection                          │
│  Number.of.items:        200                                               │
│  Source:                 Irving Berlin Estate                              │
│  Notes:                  Weeded 90 items July 91.                          │
│                                                                            │
│                                                                            │
│                          Inputter.ID                                       │
│                          Cataloger.ID                                      │
│                                                                            │
└────────────────────────────────────────────────────────────────────────────┘
```

collection name field (NAME) provides a descriptive name for each
collection so that users of the system can readily identify each collection.

These three fields are used throughout the application to
control display of and access to a given collection. The accession
number information in the ID field is placed in a hidden field in
each discographic item record to identify the collection of which
that record is a part. The *record type* field controls whether a given
collection is to be available for discographic item input. The information in the collection name field is placed in a number of places:
it is placed at the top of the discographic item data input screen
while input is done, on screen when reference access to the database is used, and on printouts of contents for individual physical
items. In each instance, the presence of the collection name serves
to identify the collection to which a given record belongs.

A number of fields in the collection entry window allow for
collection-level statistics keeping. These fields are the add date
(AD), which is the date a collection record was added to the database; the update date (UD), which is the latest date that any modi-
fications were made to the collection record; the initials of the person who input the collection record (IID); the number of items in
the collection (NOI); and, the initials of the person who cataloged
the collection (CID).

The three remaining fields are optional fields that describe a given collection more fully. They are the main entry field (ME), the source of acquisition field (SRC), and the notes field (NOTES). The main entry field was added to the file to correspond to the 1xx field in a MARC record, but thus far this field has not received much use. The source of acquisition field stores the name of the donor of the collection. The notes field provides the inputter a place to add any comments about the collection that may be needed to process the collection.

An example of the information a minimal collection level record might contain is given below:

ID: L89.01   [*Accession number*]
TR: E   [*Record type: Collection in process of Entry*]
NAME: The Toscanini Legacy Collection
                      [*Collection name/Title*]

A more complete entry for this record would include the following data:

NOI: 600 cu ft.   [*Extent of collection*]
SRC: The Toscanini Family; 1968
                       [*Source of acquisition and date*]
NOTES: Portions of collection in Music Division.
          In process of preservation, 1988. [*General notes*]

In addition to these displayed fields, the collection record has a field called the BIB record ID field (BIBID), which is a hidden field that the application maintains using a relational index. This field contains a list of the ID numbers of all the discographic records that have the current collection ID stored in them. The BIBID field is used whenever the application must perform functions at the collection level.

The Bibliographic-Item Data Entry Window

The BIB data file contains series-, discographic-, and work-level information.

When the user first accesses the BIB window, the system asks the user to select, from a pop-up list (see figure 4-2), a collec-

Figure 4–2: Pop-up to Choose Collection for Input

Collection listing Choose collection to work on.		
	*L(Special)	Collection title
1	L88.03	The Lawrence & Lee Collection
2	L89.01	The Toscanini Legacy Collection
3	L89.17	Voice of America Collection
4	L89.33	The Bell Telephone Hour
5	L90.02	Festspillene i Bergen Collection
6	L91.05	Bert Lahr Collection
7	L91.23	Radio programs from the past

tion on which to work. This pop-up list is determined by the Type of Record field (TR) in the collection record; when a collection record has type of record with a value of 'E' (meaning the collection is in the process of being Entered in the database), it will appear on this opening pop-up of the BIB data entry window. To select a collection, the user simply moves the highlight bar to the appropriate collection and presses the enter key.

This starting pop-up assigns the collection's accession number to the system variable ACCID (active collection number), which is used throughout the archival database application to control access to BIB records by collection. For example, when the user creates a new BIB record, the system automatically assigns the ACCID to that BIB record; when the user attempts to view an existing BIB record, the system first checks to see if that record's collection number matches that of the active collection. Because the user must select a collection to access the BIB window, the ACCID limits work to one collection at a time.

Figure 4–3: Bibliographic Item Data Entry Window

```
                        ─Voice of America Collection─
  ID  1192                                    AD  01-16-91   UD   03-27-91
  Main entry Chesterfield [radio program]
  Date        05-09-51   Series           Original Items: 2     New items: 1
  Notes  Source: CBS 59.


  Title                        Creator/Composer        Item Date   TMG
  Opening
  Them there eyes
  Maria Monetta
  The liar song
  Names                        Groups
  Crosby, Bing voc             John Scott Trotter Orchestra prf
  Astaire, Fred prf            Judd Collins' Rhythmaires prf
  Brewer, Theresa prf
  Carpenter, Ken ann
  Titles                       Subjects
```

Data will be entered into the BIB input window (see figure 4–3), which loosely parallels the structure of a MARC record. The first field on the BIB input window is the ID field, which is simply a system-assigned sequential number. At this ID prompt, the user can call a pop-up that lists all BIB items already input in the collection (see figure 4–4), based on the list of BIBIDs stored in the collection record. From this pop-up, the user can select one or more of these BIB records to view on screen. This allows a user to find a known item quickly in a collection and call it on-screen without knowing the ID number. If the material to be described is new to the system, the user simply presses "enter" to choose the next available ID number.

The two fields to the right of the ID field, AD and UD, are fields that display the date a record was added and when it was last updated, respectively. These dates automatically are assigned to a record by the application when a record is saved or changed, and are used for statistical purposes.

The Main Entry (ME) field correlates to the 245 field in a MARC record. Because noncommercial recordings frequently lack identifying discographic information, the data in this field often are supplied by the inputter, and not transcribed from the item. When

Figure 4–4: Pop-up of Bibliographic Items in Collection

```
┌──────────────────────Voice of America Collection──────────────────┐
│  ID                                     AD              UD          │
│ ┌────────────────────────────────────────────────────────────────┐ │
│ │              Bibliographic items in the collection:             │ │
│ │           Voice of America Collection. *L(Special) 89.17.       │ │
│ │ ┌──┬────────────────────────────────────────────────┬────┬─────┐ │
│ │ │ID│Main entry                                       │Date│Order│ │
│ │ ├──┼─────────────────────────────────────────────────┼────┼─────┤
│79>1192│Chesterfield [radio program]                    │05-09-51│   │
│80│1193│Chesterfield [radio program]                    │05-23-51│   │
│81│1194│Chesterfield [radio program]                    │05-30-51│   │
│82│1195│Bohuslav Martinu program                        │03-24-52│   │
│83│1197│Boston Symphony Orchestra concert               │04-21-45│   │
│84│1198│Boston Symphony Orchestra concert               │12-22-45│   │
│85│1200│Boston Symphony Orchestra concert               │12-29-45│   │
│86│1201│Boston Symphony Orchestra concert               │01-12-46│   │
│87│1202│Boston Symphony Orchestra concert               │01-19-46│   │
│88│1203│Boston Symphony Orchestra concert               │03-16-46│   │
│89│1204│Boston Symphony Orchestra concert               │03-23-46│   │
│90│1205│Boston Symphony Orchestra concert               │03-30-46│   │
│91│1206│Boston Symphony Orchestra concert               │04-06-46│   │
                                                    └─── pg 7/7? ──┘
```

this occurs, the Main Entry closely resembles a uniform title heading. Examples of main entries are:

> "La forza del destino (1974: Milan)"

and

> "Chesterfield (Radio program)"

It should be noted that the Main Entry field does not include any names associated with a title. In order to index the creator of a work as a name, the name is placed in the NAE field (see below) as the first name in the list, along with a relator code that identifies the name as the creator of the work in the Main Entry field. The system then can add this name programmatically to the title portion of the main entry at later points.

Following this field is the Main Entry Date (MED) field, which contains the date for a discographic item as a whole, if there is one and it is known. An example of this might be the date that a political speech was given. This date is used in output processes to sort a collection chronologically and is programmatically added to the Main Entry field to help identify each discographic record more fully.

The Series field (SER) is a one character field that allows a collection to be subdivided into series in a finding aid, if necessary. By inputting values in the Series field, a collection's main listing in the finding aid can be arranged into series. When the finding aid program creates the main listing, it sorts the selected collection first by series and then alphabetically by main entry and finally by date. Two common series that are regularly employed at the Archives are "Test pressings" and "Commercial recordings." Analytic entries in the finding aid refer the user to the appropriate series in the main list. For example, a test pressing of Leo Reisman performing *Have You Got Any Castles, Baby?* would include the following cross reference in the names list:

> Reisman, Leo
> >   SEE:
> Test pressings. Have you got any castles, baby?

The next two fields, the Original Items and New Items fields, display a count of the number of physical item records that are attached to the current BIB record. These are compiled from the associated ITEM records themselves and are updated each time an ITEM record is created or changed.

The Notes field (NOTES) is used for any MARC 5xx-type notes that apply, with the exception of the contents or performer notes. This is a text field that can take an unlimited number of notes. Contents and performer notes do not need to be input here, because the system can supply them based on other fields in the database (see below for details). Any notes that might be added to a MARC record can be added here.

The Title (TI), Creator/Composer (CR), and Timing (TMG) fields replace the 505 contents note in a MARC record. Instead of inputting contents in a note, and then retyping each heading to provide analytic added entries, the user need only type in the contents information once, placing title, composer, and timing information in separate fields. The system can reformat these separate fields into a formatted note on request and place them in the appropriate area of a display of the record. By using separate fields for the constituent elements in a contents note, it becomes possible to create analytic added entries for the works listed in the contents without re-entering the names and titles, because the fields can be rearranged as needed into added entries and be indexed as names and titles. The Date (ADT) field in this area is a calculated field based on date information from an obsolete database format. User input is no longer allowed here.

The Names (NAE), Groups (CAE), Other titles (TAE), and Subjects (SAE) fields provide added entry access to BIB records; each field can contain as many entries as are needed. These fields correspond to MARC 700, 710 and 6XX fields, respectively. The Archives regularly has included relator codes where applicable (or known) with any added entry entered in the database in order to give the greatest detail possible. The application automatically places these headings in their appropriate order and format in various displays; in addition, the system can provide full analytic access for these headings.

The Physical-Item Data Entry Window

The ITEM entry window is two screens long. The first screen is devoted to physical description and processing, and content designation, while the second screen is devoted to tracking transfer information and preservation activities. The overall layout of the window proceeds from the most basic data requirements to the most detailed (see figures 4–5 and 4–6).

The minimal ITEM record can consist of an ID, an add date, a BIBID, and the fixed field physical description information. These

Figure 4–5: Physical Item Data Entry Window: Screen 1

```
┌─────────────────────────Voice of America Collection────────────────────────┐
│                       ─Entry Window for Single Items─                        │
│ PAGE 1 OF 2.   BIBID numbers:  1191, 1192                                    │
│ ID 17945                OID AC     ST  T     AD  01-18-91     UD  03-27-91   │
│ Main entry     Chesterfield [radio program], 05-02-51.  Chesterfield [radio │
│                program], 05-09-51.                                           │
│                                                                              │
│ General Physical Description:                                                │
│       KM T   OR P   Base Y  Coat M  Size D  Speed O  SND M  CAP E  RC A      │
│       KC N   GRV N  WID M   TC   B  Classmark.number  6913                   │
│    Condition         CID  Cond.Date       Treatment       TID  Treat.Date    │
│                                                                              │
│                                                                              │
│ Contents:                                                                    │
│   Control #  Title                           Title additions      TMG        │
│   1191XTI1   Opening                                             00:00       │
│   1191XTI2   Sparrow in the tree top                            03:24       │
│   1191XTI3   Lovely Senorita, qui sac                           07:30       │
│   1191XTI4   Once upon a nickel                                 19:50       │
│   1191XTI5   Mockingbird Hill                                   24:17       │
│   1192XTI1   Opening                                            30:00       │
└─ ─ ─ ─ ─ ─ ─ ─ ─ ─ ─ ─ ─ ─ ─ ─ ─ ─ ─ ─ ─ ─ ─ ─ ─ ─ ─ ─ ─ ─ ─ ─ ─ ─ ─ ─ ┘
```

Figure 4–6: Physical Item Data Entry Window: Screen 2

```
┌─────────────────────────Voice of America Collection────────────────────────┐
│ ─ ─ ─ ─ ─ ─ ─ ─ ─Entry Window for Single Items─ ─ ─ ─ ─ ─ ─ ─ ─ ─           │
│ PAGE 2 OF 2.   BIBID numbers:  1191, 1192                                    │
│ Transfer Information:                                                         │
│ Transfer source ID   2733            Transfer source classmarks *LJ-16 5108  │
│                      2734                                       *LJ-16 5109  │
│                      2735                                       *LJ-16 5110  │
│ Tape used A          Transfer eng  AC          Transfer date  01-18-91       │
│                                                                              │
│ Phono preamp N       Input N  Channel N  Turnover N/A      Rolloff  N/A      │
│ Phono EQ-Rumble  N/A           Phono EQ-High  N            Stylus  N         │
│                                                                              │
│ Equalization:        Unit:        Freq  Type  Bandwidth  Amount              │
│                                                                              │
│                                                                              │
│                                                                              │
│ Technical Notes:                                                             │
│ Playback Eq for 5-9-51 is 500/-5.                                           │
│ Stored tails out.                                                            │
│ 1k and 10k test tone at head.                                               │
└──────────────────────────────────────────────────────────────────────────┘
```

fields are in the top half of the first screen of the ITEM window.
Below these are fields that allow inputters to track condition and
treatment information.

Following the condition and treatment fields are detailed
contents fields. These allow the researcher to identify exactly which
works on the linked discographic item(s) can be found on the current item. The manner in which contents are added to item records
is described more fully below. In a closed-stack situation this is
quite important, because the archives user must be able to request
the correct work and correct item accurately (see example given

above). Detailed contents also are important for the playback personnel so that they can quickly locate a user's request from the information on the item. Providing for contents at the item level allows this.

The second screen is used only when a preservation item is created. It contains fields that allow all the necessary information concerning the transfer process to be captured. This includes information about the type of tape used, the transfer engineer, and the transfer source, as well as the settings on any signal processing equipment that was used to create a preservation tape. By including this information in the item record for preservation transfers, the system allows quick, full, and accurate documentation of how a preservation transfer was created, which can then be recreated if necessary.

The top of the first page of the item input window contains several calculated fields for informational purposes (see figure 4–5). These fields, in order on screen are: the BIBID numbers field, which displays the ID numbers of any discographic records linked to the current item; the record status field (ST), which indicates the editing and output status of the given record; the record added field (AD), which displays the date an item record was created; and the record updated field (UD), which displays the last date that an item record was changed.

The Item ID field is the first field in the ITEM window to which the user has access. Like the BIBID field, this is a system-assigned sequential number. If a given discographic record already has item records attached to it, the system automatically places these records into a short list of active records, called a *browse list*, through which the user can cycle. In addition, the user can call a pop-up that lists all ITEM records in the browse list (see figure 4–7), from which the user can select a specific ITEM record to view on screen. If the user presses the enter key at the ID prompt, the next available ID number will be assigned by the system.

Figure 4–7: Pop-up for Physical Items Linked to BIB Record

ID listing popup	
Classmark	ID
1>*LJ-16 5110 >	2735
2 *LJ-16 5111	2736
3 *LT-10 6913	17945

The operator ID field (OID) stores the initials of the person inputting or editing the item record, and automatically defaults to the initials of the inputter who logged on to *AREV*.

The Main Entry field displays the main entry of any linked discographic records. This main entry information is derived directly from the linked discographic records. If the current item is linked to more than one discographic record, each of the Main Entry fields will be displayed in the order that the user defines.

The fields on the two lines below the words "General Physical Description" are, with the exception of the classmark number field, one-character fields that mostly correspond to the 007 fixed field data in a MARC record. The individual bytes in the 007 have been set up in this application as separate fields to simplify development and programming. As discussed above, each of these fields has a pop-up of available options that is context-sensitive, based on the value of the KM field (see figure 4–8 for the Kind of Material pop-up). These fields and their descriptions are: the Kind of Material field (KM), which uses MARC values for recordings, motion pictures and videorecordings where possible; the Base Material (BASE) and Coating Material (COAT) fields, which are locally-developed fields that allow identification of particularly fragile or unstable materials in the Archives; the Size (SZ), Reproduction

Figure 4–8: Pop-up Example for Physical Description Fields (KM is shown)

Kind of Material		
	Value	Description
1>	A	Beta video
2	B	VHS video
3	C	U-matic video
4	D	Disc
5	E	Cylinder
6	G	Cartridge
7	I	Sound film reel
8	M	Motion picture
9	S	Cassette
10	T	Tape reel
11	W	Wire
12	Z	Other

Speed (SPD), Playback Channels (SND), Recording Capture (CAP), Reproduction Characteristics (RC), Kind of Cutting (KC), Groove-Type (GRV), Tape Width (WID), and Track Configuration (TC) fields, which are all derived from MARC specifications, primarily MARC for sound recordings.

The last field in this area is the Classmark Number field (CLASS), which stores the unique portion of the Archives' classmark number for the item described. The Archives uses a classmark system that is based on the format of an item. Each classmark consists of a format-derived prefix followed by a unique sequential number. Because of this, it is possible for the system to generate the format-specific prefix from the fixed-field data in the record. Thus the user only needs to input the unique number portion of the classmark; the system adds the prefix when it is needed.

The next area of the ITEM window is devoted to keeping track of condition and treatment information. The Condition (CND) field stores condition information in encoded form. The user may select from a pop-up window as many condition descriptor codes from a pop-up window as apply. Once the appropriate codes have been assigned, the user's initials and the date of the condition check must be input. These fields can be repeated, should subsequent condition surveys be carried out. The treatment fields function in the same way as the condition fields, tracking any treatments that may have been performed on an item.

The contents area allows the inputter to select detailed contents information for a given physical item from a pop-up that lists all the works on all the discographic records linked to an item. The Title Additions field allows special contents information to be recorded that results strictly from physical limitations. An example of this might be when a preservation tape contains only a portion of an act of an opera. This field allows information such as this, which is a result of the physical format, to be tracked without affecting the discographic record. The Timing field in this window allows the archives to capture location timings on a given physical item. Once these fields are filled out by transfer engineers, a detailed cue sheet can be printed out that lists individual works and their timings and locations on the preservation item (see figure 4–9). This contents information also is needed by playback engineers to enable them to locate a requested work on a set of tapes.

Should any given physical item contain recorded material from more than one discographic item—for example, a preservation transfer that contains two radio program episodes—the inputter manually can link one physical-item record to more than one discographic item record. This process is accessible at any time in the item window, although it is most frequently invoked when the inputter reaches the contents area. The user is first prompted for the discographic ID number to which the current item is to be linked (see figure 4–10, step 1), after which the user must select the order in which the discographic records appear on the physical item (see figure 4–10, step 2).

The second screen of the item window (see figure 4–6), the transfer documentation screen, like the first screen, lists the currently linked discographic records at the top. Directly below this are fields that list the item ID numbers and the item classmarks for the original source material for the preservation item. The transfer

Figure 4–9: Technical Data Sheet for Physical Item

The Rodgers & Hammerstein Archives of Recorded Sound
The New York Public Library at Lincoln Center
111 Amsterdam Avenue
New York, NY 10023

Chesterfield [radio program], 05-02-51 -- Chesterfield [radio program], 05-09-51.

1 sound tape reel, 7 1/2 ips ; 10 in.

Detailed bibliographic information:

Chesterfield [radio program], 05-02-51.
Source: CBS 59.
Other entries: Bing Crosby, Burt Wheeler, Walter Okeefe, Ken Carpenter, John
Scott Trotter Orchestra, Judd Collins' Rhythmaires.
AREV ID: 1191.

Chesterfield [radio program], 05-09-51.
Source: CBS 59.
Other entries: Bing Crosby, Fred Astaire, Theresa Brewer, Ken Carpenter,
John Scott Trotter Orchestra, Judd Collins' Rhythmaires.
AREV ID: 1192.

Forms part of: Voice of America Collection. Finding aid in: *L(Special) 89-17.

Figure 4–9: (continued)

Title, Creator/Composer, and date	Timing
Chesterfield [radio program], 05-02-51:	
Opening.	00:00
Sparrow in the tree top.	03:24
Lovely Senorita, qui sac.	07:30
Once upon a nickel.	19:50
Mockingbird Hill.	24:17
Chesterfield [radio program], 05-09-51:	
Opening.	30:00
Them there eyes.	32:32
Maria Monetta.	35:43
The liar song.	40:18
Never been kissed.	50:15
From the bottom of my heart.	54:41

TRANSFER SOURCE:

Originals in: *LJ-16 5108, *LJ-16 5109, *LJ-16 5110, *LJ-16 5111.
Original items description: 4 sound discs : analog, 33 1/3 rpm, aluminum-based acetate ; 16 in.

TECHNICAL NOTES:

Phono preamp: Owl 1.
Input level: -20 dB.   Input channel: Mono (L + R).   Turnover: 750 Hz.   Rolloff: 8.5 dB.
Rumble filter: 40 Hz.   H. F. Filter: 18K kHz.
Stylus used: 1.5TE.

Play back Eq for 5-9-51 is 500/-5.
Stored tails out.
1k and 10k test tone at head.
1k = 0VU @ 250 nWb/m.
Transfer engineer: XXXXXX XXXXXXXXX.   Transfer date: 01-18-91.

Figure 4–10: Screens to Link One Physical Item to Multiple Bibliographic Records.

Step 1:

```
┌──────────────Popup for linking Item records──────────────┐
│                                                           │
│  What is the BIB ID you wish to link to?                  │
│  Type the ID or press <F2> for a list:                    │
│                                                           │
└───────────────────────────────────────────────────────────┘
```

Step 2:

	ID	Main entry	Date	Order
		Bibliographic records currently linked to this item – Select records in order on item		
1>	1192	Chesterfield [radio program]	05-09-51	2
2	1193	Chesterfield [radio program]	05-02-51	1

source ID field contains the item ID numbers for the original source material. From this field the user can select original item records from a pop-up that lists all these items. The transfer source classmark field is a calculated field that displays the classmarks of any original items selected in the transfer source ID field. These fields cannot be filled in if the item being described is an original item; the system checks the original vs. reproduction field in the record before allowing input.

The tape used field is a one-byte field that allows the user to specify the brand of tape used for a transfer. Because different brands of tape often behave differently over time, this field was added to allow these data to be tracked for future needs. The user can select the brand of tape used from a pop-up. The transfer engineer and the transfer date fields are used for statistics-keeping purposes.

The phono preamp settings fields follow. These fields store information about the preamp used and its settings for disc playback. Because noncommercial sound recordings often have used variant recording curves, the appropriate settings, once found by playback or transfer personnel, should be captured for future play-back. The fields allow each aspect of a standard phono preamp to be identified; in most cases, this is accomplished by using one-byte codes. Each coded field has its own table-based pop-up. If the item being described doesn't use a phono preamp, these fields are set to 'N' (Not applicable).

In developing the phono preamp settings portion of the item input screen, an interesting fact arose: in order to determine the phono preamp settings for a given recording, it had to be played. However, when most of these original items were being played, they were being played for transfer, and the item record on screen was the record for the preservation item, for which special playback curves did not apply. Furthermore, for most sets of discs, the preamp settings would be the same, even if there were seven or ten physical items. Adding the same settings to all the item records af-ter the fact would be cumbersome, because each item record would have to be edited individually. A pop-up window (see figure 4–11) was created that allowed the engineer to input the settings for all the original items for a given transfer item, which then updates each original item with the appropriate information. This window is accessible from anywhere in the window, but will only display if there are item IDs listed in the source field.

Figure 4-11: Phono Preamp Input Window

```
┌──────────Phono Preamp Input Window──────────┐
│                                              │
│   Phono.preamp         Input                 │
│   Channel              Turnover              │
│   Rolloff              Phono.EQ-Rumble       │
│   Phono.EQ-High        Stylus                │
│                                              │
└──────────────────────────────────────────────┘
```

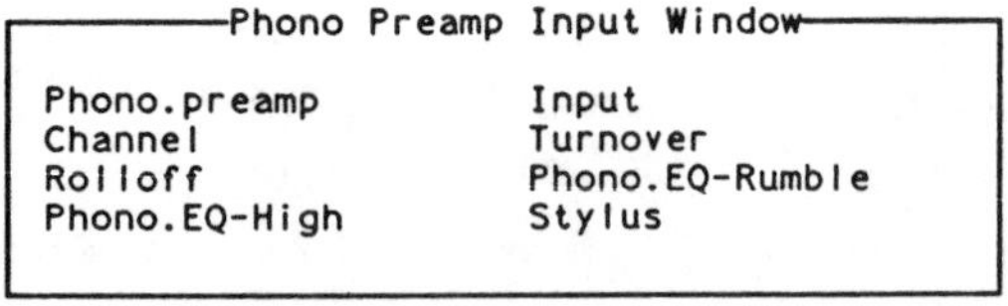

The equalization section allows the engineer to note any spe-cific signal processing units used and the settings on them. In order to accommodate the wide variety of units that might be used at the Archives, an input protocol was established whereby each band of equalization in any unit would be listed separately, listing the unit, the frequency of the processing, the basic type of processing, the band-width of the effect, and the amount of processing used. While this method is not as intuitive as establishing fields that duplicate a unit's knobs, the number of signal processing units that have been used, are used, and will be used at the Archives are too great to allow this. Because the majority of signal processing units have these four basic facets to them, it was decided to use this modular approach. In practice the system has not proven too cumbersome for our engineers.

The final field in the item window is a general notes field that allows transfer engineers to add any further information about the transfer process that was not reflected in other fields. This field might be used to document any extraordinary steps taken to achieve a given transfer, such as using a lubricant to quiet surface noise on a disc, or the varying playback speeds used.

Conclusion

This detailed description of the archival sound recordings database presented fields in the order in which they would be encountered by a user working on an archival sound recording collection. In the final chapter we will consider ways in which this database might continue to evolve.

Note

1. In *Advanced Revelation* a real data field stores actual data; a symbolic field is calculated by the program.

Chapter 5: Into the Future

Introduction

The Archival Sound Recordings Database is a working technical services database. It meets many of the needs of the Archives staff members and public users. Primary among these are the need for highly detailed, work-level finding aids; physical item-specific condition information; and accurate documentation of preservation transfer activities. The database serves these functions while at the same time allowing simplified data input and processing. This simplification speeds processing time immensely and makes complex data-tracking comprehensible to more users. In this chapter we consider future plans for the application.

The Future

The Archival Sound Recordings Database is far from a completed database. As work continues on the processing of the Archives' materials, it has become clear that a number of major enhancements to the system would be desirable, particularly to make the database more efficient to search and easier to add to. Among these are a linked authority file, a user-interface for the public, an integrated link to the library's online catalog, and the ability to handle other formats of archival material. In fact, work on some of these enhancements has begun already.

Linked Authority File

A linked authority file is the most important of these features. Most of the initial documentation for the archival sound recordings materials is being created by the transfer engineers who listen to the recordings as they transfer collections to stable media. However, the engineers are not trained to use uniform headings to describe these collections; consequently, variant headings spring up in the system rapidly. Correcting these headings takes a great deal of librarian time.

By using a linked authority file and requiring engineers to derive headings directly from that authority file, the chances of variant headings are cut drastically, and editing time can be reduced. Instead of forcing transfer engineers to create standardized headings from scratch each time, a linked authority file would allow them simply to choose the correct heading from already existing authority records. Using a linked authority file also limits the number of mistyped headings, because the headings are not stored in each discographic record but are imported from the authority file. Because the headings are stored only once in the authority file, changing a heading from one form to another also becomes a much quicker procedure.

One aspect of an authority file that is especially complicated in the noncommercial sound recordings database is the fact that the database merges the descriptive portion of a discographic record with the access points portion. Initially, this didn't seem to be too critical, because most of the data being captured in the database were not transcribed. It was more efficient to capture contents data once and use those data both for descriptive contents and for analytic added entries. However, difficulties begin to arise when an authorized access point is required for indexing but a variant heading would be more useful for description.

An example of this is a popular song that is from a musical. A standard authority heading for the song would include the composer of the musical and its title, followed by the individual song title. If the song is performed in the course of a recording of the whole musical, however, repeatedly displaying the composer and musical title for each song would be extremely redundant and distracting. For example, if a recording of Jerome Kern's musical *Showboat* were to use authority headings without modification for all of its contents, the contents note would appear as the following:

> Contents: Showboat. Overture / Jerome Kern — Showboat. Cotton blossom / Jerome Kern — Showboat. Only make believe / Jerome Kern — Showboat. Ol' man river / Jerome Kern — Showboat. Can't help lovin' dat man / Jerome Kern — Showboat. Life upon the wicked stage / Jerome Kern — Showboat. You are my love / Jerome Kern — Showboat. Why do I love you? / Jerome Kern — Showboat. Bill / Jerome Kern — Showboat. Nobody else but me / Jerome Kern.

Furthermore, storing the musical title in the authority record for each song can become very cumbersome. Ultimately, some solution must be found that allows only specific (and possibly specified) portions of a heading to be displayed at certain times.

Nevertheless, a rudimentary authority file already has been established, and initial attempts to link this authority file to the discographic file have been carried out. The authority file, insofar as it goes, which admittedly is not far, follows MARC authority structures. The main heading field is provided with tags, indicators, and some subfields; additionally, there are fields for cross references and status codes. Inputters can search this file and import the authorized heading into the discographic record. In the future, the discographic record will store only pointers to authority file records.

Online Public Access

The second feature that is needed is a user interface that will allow public access to the database. Such a user interface will require display screens that the public can understand, and that preferably follow established local or national standards for displays. It would include clear and simple searching functions, with help screens for the novice user and perhaps a command-line interface for experienced users. An option might be added to allow the user to configure the data as needed on screen. The system would allow the user to export the data in either printed or online form.

Initial attempts have been made to add this feature. A display-only window has been created that allows searching access for reference staff. From this screen reference users can search in any of the indexes for the file and see a display of the search results. The data that are displayed cannot be edited by the user. While the index structure is limited in its scope, it does allow the user to search almost any data area of the individual discographic records, thus making all of the processed archival sound recordings immediately available to the reference staff. There is no flexibility in the display in this reference window; the user can see a record only in a card layout. Furthermore, there is no formal method of exporting the data found, in either printed or electronic form. Obviously, for a truly user-accessible database, these issues will have to be addressed in more depth.

Links to an Online Catalog

The third feature needed is a direct link to the library's online catalog, so that users searching for a certain name will get a positive result if the name appears anywhere in the archival database. Thus, if a person searches for Winston Churchill in the online catalog, the A.F.R. Lawrence collection-level MARC record would be among the search results. The search would return the collection record in order to give the researcher an overview of the collection, and also because of the presence of the collection-level MARC-AMC record already in the online catalog. Some method would have to be established to allow the analytic added entries to point to the MARC-AMC record, without actually adding these headings, because placing every added entry in the MARC-AMC record would overload most online catalogs (see below). The index structure needed to support this feature would have to be somewhat complex for this to be possible.

Once the user had made an initial search and had determined that the archival collection was the best record to follow up, a "hot-key" would give access to individual records within an archival collection. Preferably, this hot-key access would allow for different types of display, and would include only those records in the collection that have the heading for which the user had searched without having to repeat the search in the archival database.

In order to carry out this unified database system, a great number of details must be worked out. Coordinating the indexing between the MARC database and the archival database is perhaps the most difficult. Reconciling the conflicting data structures between the MARC database and the archival sound recordings database is a second major problem, because the local database uses separate data files and records for what is described in single records in MARC. A third major problem is establishing the details of the user interface.

The simplest solution to the indexing issue is to transfer all analytic headings from the archival database directly into the MARC record. Then, when a user searches for a specific name or title heading, the MARC-AMC record will be found and displayed. This, however, will result in MARC records that exceed most systems' record-length limitations. These records, moreover, could not be viewed realistically in an online catalog (imagine a MARC record with 600 name-added entries . . .), because the records would be so lengthy.

A second way to give access to these data is to import the archival database in its entirety into the online catalog as a special database. Then the user would be able to search the database in addition to the usual MARC database. This solution is complicated by the multi-level structure of the archival database; some decisions would have to be made about how to modify the record structure to fit the online catalog's data structure. Most likely, the database would have to be converted to some sort of MARC structure.

Any joined access and display of the two data structures would have to be coordinated so that the user could understand easily the different systems without difficulty. Most probably, the data from the archival database would have to mimic the displays of the online catalog. However, it might be necessary to add other types of displays for archival materials. For example, it might be important to give the user broader views of the data or to prevent the casual user from requesting rare and fragile materials when more common or stable materials will suffice.

Adding Format Flexibility

Another desirable feature is the descriptive flexibility to allow a wider range of archival material to be processed in the system. The ideal database structure would allow all types of material to be described, not just sound recordings and visual materials. As Fox states, "a collection might contain items in only a single physical format or many;"[1] archival collections rarely are organized by format and therefore the database should accommodate descriptions of material in formats other than those that are strictly audiovisual in nature.

This feature can be added at some future date without serious impact on the database because of the current database's reliance on tables to determine descriptive limitations. In order to validate new formats in the database, the table records for the physical item file will have to be updated and formatting programs modified to handle these new data. Some aspects of the physical item data file will have to be interpreted or omitted altogether, for example, the fields that deal specifically with the physical characteristics of a sound recording. Finally, descriptive standards will have to be established to ensure that the different types of archival material are described in the most sensible and useful manner.

Conclusion

The noncommercial sound recordings database is a database that allows the Archives to process special collection materials more rapidly than could have been imagined before. By using a database program to capture item-level information in an archival entity it has become possible to give highly detailed data to users on a timely basis, without necessarily losing the overview of the archival entity.

The database that has arisen from the Archives' needs is far from perfect, but it meets many of those needs adequately. It keeps track of detailed contents information; it facilitates preservation transfer activities; and it gives the public some access to these materials from both the macro and micro levels. The database provides all of the Archives' users with information that generally was not available before, thus furthering the Archives' mission.

Reference

1. Michael J. Fox. "Descriptive Cataloging for Archival Materials," *Cataloging and Classification Quarterly* 11, no. 3/4 (1990), 21.

Appendix A: Data Elements in the Archival Sound Recordings Database

Field*	MARC Equivalent

COLLECTION DATA FILE

In the COLLECTION file all fields are variable-length text fields (i.e. fields that will allow input of any amount of information in any format) except where noted.

ID	001, 090 $b

The ID field is derived from the collection accession number and serves as both the record control number and the collection's call number.

NAME (Title)	245
ME (Main entry)	100
SRC (Source) 541 $a	
TR (Type of record)	N/A

Fixed-length field that controls subsequent processing of a collection.

Codes
A	Accession-level record
E	Entry-window record
F	Finished collection
P	Manually-processed collection

NOI (Number of items)	541 $n, 300
NOTES	5XX

---

*There are no subfields defined in the Archival Sound Recordings Database.

Field	MARC Equivalent
AD (Add date)	005
UD (Update date)	005
IID (Inputter's initials)	N/A
CID (Cataloger's initials)	N/A
BIBIDS (Discographic item IDs)	N/A

BIB DATA FILE

In the BIB file all fields are variable-length text fields except where noted.

ID	001
ME (Main entry)	1XX

The ME (main entry) field contains only title information; if a name is associated with a given title, then it is placed in the NAE field and programmatically linked to the title to create the heading as needed.

MED (Main entry date)	033

Formatted date field. Input in the form: MM-DD-YY.

SER (Series)	4XX

Fixed-length field that assigns a BIB record to a given series. Values can be defined on a collection-by-collection basis, although the following values are recommended for common types of series.

Codes

A	Test pressing
B	Commercial recording
2	Copy 2
3	Copy 3

NOTES	5XX, except 505, 511

Field	MARC Equivalent
TI	505, 7XX title portions
CR	505, 7XX name portions
ADT	033

Formatted date field. Input in the form:
MM-DD-YY.
   OBSOLETE.

TMG	306, 505 durations

Formatted timings. Input in the form: MM:SS.

NAE	700 $a
CAE	710 $a
TAE	730, 740
SAE	6XX
ACCID	N/A

System-assigned linking field that contains
the accession record control number for a
BIB record.

ITEM DATA FILE

ID	001

Control number for physical item record.
Assigned by system.

OID	N/A

Fixed field for operator's initials.

ST	N/A

Fixed field for record status.

TECHNOTES	N/A

Variable-length field for adding information
not included in other fields.

AD	005

Date record was added to database.

UD	005

Date of most recent transaction on record.

Field	**MARC Equivalent**

CLASSPREFIX   090 $b

Classmark prefix of item. Contains only first portion of classmark, which is derived from format of item. System- generated.

CLASS   090 $b

Classmark number of item. Contains only second portion of classmark.

BIBID   N/A

Contains record control number for linked records in the BIB file.

KM   007/01SR

Fixed field for kind of material (i.e. format)   007/04VM

of a given physical item. Used by applica-   007/01MP

tion to control content of subsequent fields.

Codes

A	Videocassette (Beta)
B	Videocassette (VHS)
C	Videocassette (U-matic)
D	Sound disc
E	Sound cylinder
G	Cartridge
I	Sound film reel
M	Film reel
S	Sound cassette
T	Sound tape reel
W	Sound wire recording
Z	Other

O.R   007/02SR

Fixed field for original versus reproduction   007/02VM

aspect of item. This field has been modified   007/02MP

for local use.

Field	**MARC Equivalent**

Codes

F	Facsimile
O	Original item
P	Preservation copy item
R	Reproduction
S	Service copy item
U	Unknown

BASE   007/12MP

Fixed field for base material of item.

Codes

A	Acetate
D	Safety (diacetate)
G	Glass
I	Nitrate
L	Aluminum
M	Mixed base
P	Paper
S	Shellac
V	Plastic/vinyl
W	Wax
Y	Polyester
O	Other
U	Unknown

Table Of Values Valid For Each Value Of KM

KM Value	Valid Values of Current Field
A	A, P, V, Y, O, U
B	A, P, V, Y, O, U
C	A, P, V, Y, O, U
D	G, L, P, S, V, O, U
E	S, V, W, O, U

Field		MARC Equivalent
G	A, P, V, Y, O, U	
I	D, M, N, V, O, U	
M	D, M, N, V, O, U	
S	A, P, V, Y, O, U	
T	A, P, V, Y, O, U	
W	O	
Z	All codes	

COAT   N/A

Fixed field for coating material of item.

Codes

A	Acetate
M	Magnetic
N	No coating
W	Wax
U	Unknown
Z	Other

Table Of Values Valid For Each Value Of KM

KM Value	Valid Values of Current Field
A	M
B	M
C	M
D	A, N, W, U, Z
E	N
G	M
I	N
M	N
S	M
T	M
W	N
Z	All codes

Field	**MARC Equivalent**
SZ	007/06SR

Fixed field for dimension of item.

Codes

A	3 inches
B	5 inches
C	7 inches
D	10 inches
E	12 inches
F	16 inches
G	4 3/4 inches
J	Cassette
K	6 inches
L	8 inches
M	13 inches
N	Not applicable
O	Cartridge (5 1/4 x 3 7/8)
S	Cylinder
U	Unknown
Z	Other

Table Of Values Valid For Each Value Of KM

KM Value	Valid Values of Current Field
A	N
B	N
C	N
D	A, B, K, C, L, D, E, M, F, G, Z
E	S
G	N
I	N
M	N
S	J

Field   **MARC Equivalent**

T	A, B, C, D, U, Z
W	N
Z	All codes

SPD   007/03SR

Fixed field for reproduction speed of item.

Codes

A	16 rpm
B	33 1/3 rpm
C	45 rpm
D	78 rpm
E	8 rpm
H	120 rpm
I	160 rpm
K	15/16 ips
L	1 7/8 ips
M	3 3/4 ips
N	Not applicable
O	7 1/2 ips
P	15 ips
R	30 ips
U	Unknown
Z	Other

Table Of Values Valid For Each Value Of KM

KM Value	Valid Values of Current Field
A	N
B	N
C	N
D	A, B, C, D, U, Z
E	H, I, U, Z
G	N

Field		MARC Equivalent
I	N	
M	N	
S	L	
T	K, L, M, N, O, P, R, U, Z	
W	U	
Z	All codes	

SND		007/04SR
Fixed field for configuration of playback		007/08VM
channels of item.		007/08MP

Codes

K	Mixed
M	Monophonic
N	Not applicable
Q	Quadraphonic
S	Stereophonic
U	Unknown
Z	Other

Table Of Values Valid For Each Value Of KM

KM Value	Valid Values of Current Field
A	All codes
B	All codes
C	All codes
D	All codes
E	M
G	All codes
I	All codes
M	All codes
S	All codes
T	All codes
W	M
Z	All codes

Field	**MARC Equivalent**
CAP	007/13SR

Fixed field for capture and storage technique
of item.

Codes

A	Acoustical capture, direct storage
B	Direct storage, not acoustical
D	Digital storage
E	Analog electrical storage
U	Unknown
Z	Other capture

RC	007/12SR

Fixed field for special playback characteristics
of item.

Codes

A	NAB standard
B	CCIR standard
C	Dolby-B encoded
D	dbx encoded
E	Digital recording
F	Dolby-A encoded
G	Dolby-C encoded
H	CX encoded
N	Not applicable
U	Unknown
Z	Other

Table Of Values Valid For Each Value Of KM

KM Value	Valid Values of Current Field
A	All codes
B	All codes
C	All codes

Field	MARC Equivalent
D	A, B, E, H, N, U, Z
E	N, U, Z
G	All codes
I	All codes
M	All codes
S	All codes
T	All codes
W	U
Z	All codes

KC   007/11SR

Fixed field for kind of cutting in item.

Codes

H	Hill and dale
L	Lateral or combined
N	Not applicable
U	Unknown

Table Of Values Valid For Each Value Of KM

KM Value	Valid Values of Current Field
A	N
B	N
C	N
D	L, H, U
E	L, H, U
G	N
I	N
M	N
S	N
T	N
W	N
Z	All codes

Field	**MARC Equivalent**
GRV	007/05SR

Fixed field for groove width/groove pitch
of item.

Codes

M	Microgroove
N	Not applicable
S	Coarse/Standard
U	Unknown
Z	Other groove width

Table Of Values Valid For Each Value Of Km

KM Value	Valid Values of Current Field
A	N
B	N
C	N
D	S, M, U, Z
E	S, M, U, Z
G	N
I	N
M	N
S	N
T	N
W	N
Z	All codes

WID	007/07SR
	007/07VM
	007/07MP

Fixed field for tape width of item.

Codes

A	Standard 8 mm.
B	Super 8 mm.
C	9.5 mm.
D	16 mm.

Field   **MARC Equivalent**

E	28 mm.
F	35 mm.
L	1/8 in.
M	1/4 in.
N	Not applicable
O	1/2 in.
P	1 in.
R	3/4 in.
U	Unknown
Z	Other tape width

Table Of Values Valid For Each Value Of KM

KM Value	Valid Values of Current Field
A	L, M, O, P, R, U, Z
B	L, M, O, P, R, U, Z
C	L, M, O, P, R, U, Z
D	N
E	N
G	L, M, O, P, R, U, Z
I	A, B, C, D, E, F, U, Z
M	A, B, C, D, E, F, U, Z
S	L, M, O, P, R, U, Z
T	L, M, O, P, R, U, Z
W	N
Z	All codes

TC   007/08SR

Fixed field for track configuration of item.

Codes

A	Full track
B	Half (2) track
C	Quarter (4) track

Field		**MARC Equivalent**
D	8 track	
E	12 track	
F	16 track	
N	Not applicable	
U	Unknown	
Z	Other	

Table Of Values Valid For Each Value Of KM

KM Value	Valid Values of Current Field
A	All codes
B	All codes
C	All codes
D	N
E	N
G	All codes
I	All codes
M	All codes
S	All codes
T	All codes
W	N
Z	All codes

CND (Condition of item)   583 $i

Variable length field for identifying condition state of item.

Codes

BB	Bubbling
CH	Chipped
CK	Cracked
CZ	Crazed
CU	Curled
DN	Dented
ED	Edge damage

Field		MARC Equivalent
FK	Flaking	
FT	Fluting	
GR	Greying	
HD	Heat damage	
LD	Leadered	
LW	Loosely-wound	
NL	Non-leadered	
NF	Nitrate fading	
NO	Nitrate odor	
NS	Nitrate sticky	
OX	Oxidizing	
PK	Pancake	
PL	Peeling	
PT	Pitted	
SF	Scuffed	
SP	Splices	
ST	Scratched	
TW	Tightly-wound	
TU	Tightly-wound uneven	
WD	Withdrawn	
WP	Warped	

Table Of Values Valid For Each Value Of KM

KM Value	Valid Values of Current Field
A	CU, ED, FT, LD, LW, NL, PK, SP, TW, TU, WD
B	CU, ED, FT, LD, LW, NL, PK, SP, TW, TU, WD
C	CU, ED, FT, LD, LW, NL, PK, SP, TW, TU, WD
D	CH, CK, CZ, DN, FK, GR, HD, OX, PL, PT, SF, ST, WD, WP
E	CH, CK, CZ, DN, FK, GR, HD, OX, PL, PT, SF, ST, WD, WP
G	CU, ED, FT, LD, LW, NL, PK, SP, TW, TU, WD
I	BB, CU, ED, FK, NF, NO, NS, OX, SP, ST, WD

Field	MARC Equivalent
M	BB, CU, ED, FK, NF, NO, NS, OX, SP, ST, WD
S	CU, ED, FT, LD, LW, NL, PK, SP, TW, TU, WD
T	CU, ED, FT, LD, LW, NL, PK, SP, TW, TU, WD
W	CU, ED, FT, LD, LW, NL, PK, SP, TW, TU, WD
Z	All codes

CID (Initials of condition evaluator)	583 $k
CDT (Date of condition evaluation)	583 $c
TRT (Treatment taken)	583 $a

Variable length field for preservation
treatment of item.

Codes

MX	Monks Machine Used
MO	Mineral Oil Used
LD	Leadered
NA	Not applicable
RP	Repacking to reel
TW	Tight-wound
SR	Splices replaced
ZZ	Other

Table Of Values Valid For Each Value Of KM

KM Value	Valid Values of Current Field
A	NA, ZZ
B	NA, ZZ
C	NA, ZZ
D	MX, MO, NA, ZZ
E	NA, ZZ
G	NA, ZZ
I	NA, ZZ
M	NA, ZZ

Field		MARC Equivalent
S	NA, ZZ	
T	LD, NA, RP TW, SR, ZZ	
W	NA, ZZ	
Z	All codes	

TID (Initials of person giving treatment)	583 $k
TRTD (Date of treatment)	583 $c
TIVAL (Contents control numbers)	N/A
Contains pointer information only for contents. Actual data resides in BIB file.	
TIADD (Additions to title)	N/A
Contains textual additions to contents that are necessary only for physical reasons.	
TMG (Timings)	N/A
Contains timings that identify the location of a work on a given physical item.	
SRC (Transfer source)	583 $3
Contains record control numbers for items that contain the source recording for a preservation/service copy.	
TU (Tape used)	N/A
Fixed-length field for the brand of tape used for a preservation/service copy.	

Codes

A	Agfa 468
B	Scotch 208
C	Scotch 808
D	TDK SAX-60
E	TDK SAX-90
U	Unknown
Z	Other

Field	**MARC Equivalent**
TE (Transfer engineer)	583 $k

Initials of the person carrying out the
transfer process.

TD (Transfer date)	583 $c
PPA (Phono preamp)	N/A

Fixed-length field for the phono preamp
used for disc recording playback.

Codes

O	Owl 1
S	Stanton 310
N	Not applicable
Z	Other

PIN (Phono input level)   N/A

Codes

A	-20 dB
B	0 dB
N	Not applicable
Z	Other

PCH (Preamp channel)   N/A

Fixed-length field for the channel selection
used on playback
of disc recordings.

Codes

M	Mono (L + R)
L	Left
R	Right
S	Stereo
V	Vertical
N	Not applicable

Field	MARC Equivalent

PTURN   N/A

Fixed-length field for the turnover setting
on the phono preamp.

Codes

F	Flat
2	250 Hz
3	375 Hz
5	500 Hz
7	750 Hz
1	1 kHz
R	RIAA
N	Not applicable
Z	Other

PROLL   N/A

Fixed-length field for the rolloff setting
used.

Codes

F	Flat
5	5 dB
8	8.5 dB
2	12 dB
4	14 dB
6	16 dB
R	RIAA
O	Other
N	Not applicable

PEQR   N/A

Fixed-length field for the rumble setting
on the phono preamp.

Field   **MARC Equivalent**

Codes

2	20 Hz
3	30 Hz
4	40 Hz
5	50 Hz
6	60 Hz
7	70 Hz
1	110 Hz
B	Bypass
N	Not applicable
Z	Other

PEQH   N/A

Fixed-length field for the high filter setting
on the phono preamp. Input as the number
of kilohertz of cutoff frequency.

STY   N/A

Field for the stylus used for playback.

EQNIT   N/A

Fixed-length field for the signal processing
unit used.

Codes

A	Owl 1 Multifilter
B	Urei 565 Filter
C	Orban Parametric
D	Packburn
Z	Other

EQFQ   N/A

Fixed-length field that identifies the fre
quency at which a signal processing unit is
set.

Field		MARC Equivalent

Codes

LF	Low frequency
ML	Mid-Low frequency
MH	Mid-High frequency
HF	High frequency

EQTP   N/A

Fixed-length field for the type of signal processing used.

Codes

N	Notch
P	Peak
S	Shelve
Z	Other

EQBW   N/A

Fixed-length field for the bandwidth of the
signal processing.

Codes

N	Narrow
M	Medium
W	Wide

EQAMT   N/A

Fixed-length field for the amount of signal
processing used. Given in terms that the
unit defines.

Appendix B: Flowcharts

Archival Sound Recordings Database Structure Overview

Flowchart 1: Collection Window Overview

Flowchart 2: Finding Aid Subroutine

Flowchart 3: Collection Window Pre-Save Routine

Flowchart 4: BIB Window Overview

Flowchart 5: BIB Window Post-Initialization

Flowchart 6: BIB Window ID Popup

Flowchart 7: BIB Window Post-Read Record

Flowchart 8: BIB Window Classmark Popup

Flowchart 9: Bibliographic Record Pre-Save Routine

Flowchart 10: BIB Window Post-Save Record

Flowchart 11: ITEM Window Overview

Flowchart 12: ITEM Window Postinitialization

Flowchart 13: ITEM Window ID Popup

Flowchart 14: ITEM Window Post-Read Record

Flowchart 15: ITEM Window Pre-Prompt Routine

Flowchart 16: ITEM Window Post-Prompt Subroutine

Flowchart 17: ITEM Window Generic Popup Subroutine

Flowchart 18: ITEM Window Multi-Bib Routine

Flowchart 19: ITEM Window Unlink Routine

Flowchart 20: ITEM Window Contents Popup

Flowchart 21: ITEM Window Transfer Source Popup

Flowchart 22: ITEM Window Preamp Subroutine

Flowchart 23: Item Record Pre-Save Routine

Flowchart 24: ITEM Window Post-Save Record

Flowchart 25: ITEM Window Post-Delete Record

Archival Sound Recordings Database Structure: Overview

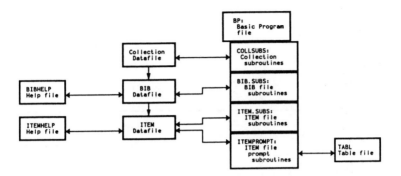

Flowchart 1: Collection Window Overview

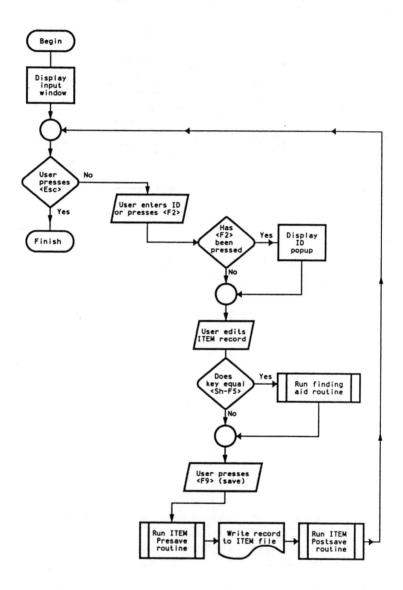

Flowchart 2: Finding Aid Subroutine

Run when user presses <Shift-F5> in collection window. Takes data from BIB file, formats it and exports it in a card and four index layouts.

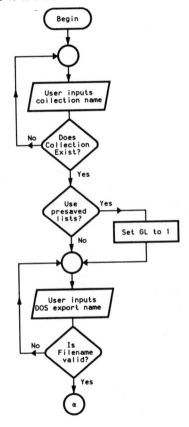

Flowchart 2 *(continued)*

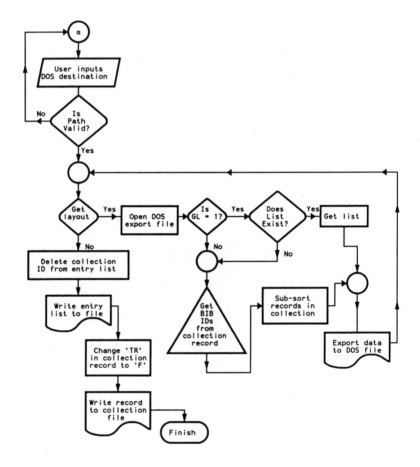

Flowchart 3: Collection Window Pre-Save Routine

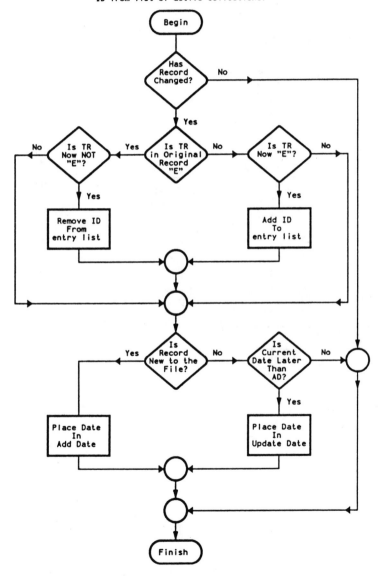

Run after user presses <F9>, but before record is written to disk.
Maintains Add date and Update date fields. Adds or removes collection
ID from list of active collections.

Flowchart 4: BIB Window Overview

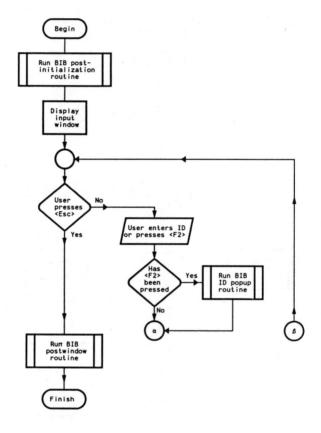

Flowchart 4 *(continued)*

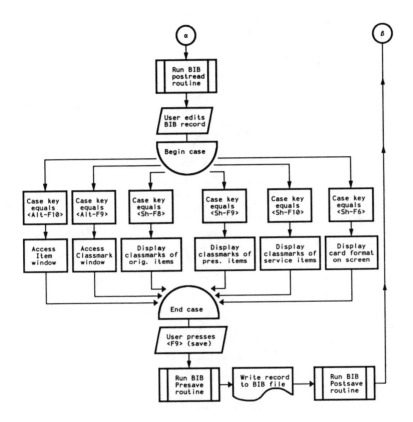

Flowchart 5: BIB Window Post-Initialization

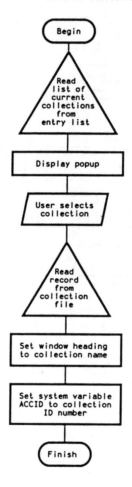

Run when user first accesses BIB window. Allows user to select a collection on which to work. Also sets system variable to selected collection ID.

Begin

Read list of current collections from entry list

Display popup

User selects collection

Read record from collection file

Set window heading to collection name

Set system variable ACCID to collection ID number

Finish

Flowchart 6: BIB Window ID Popup

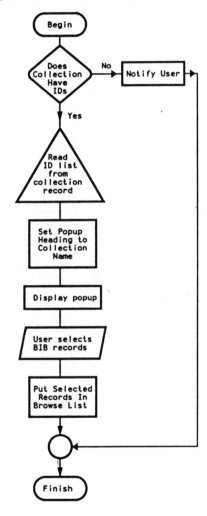

Flowchart 7: BIB Window Post-Read Record

Run after user selects a BIB record and before the record displays on screen. Verifies that chosen record is part of active collection. Sets variable BIBID to current ID number.

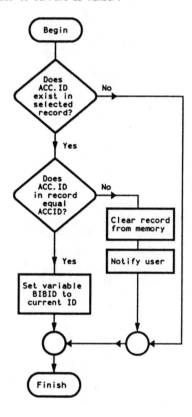

Flowchart 8: BIB Window Classmark Popup

Run when user wants to see the classmarks of items
linked to current BIB record. Depending on the key
pressed, the program displays only original items,
preservation items, or service items.

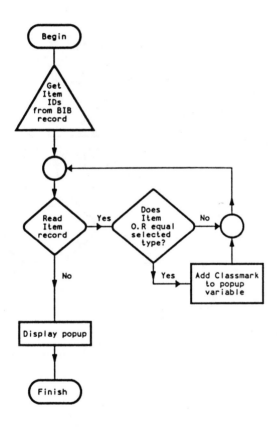

Flowchart 9: Bibliographic Record Pre-Save Routine

Run after user presses <F9>, but before the record is written to disk.
Maintains Add date and Update date fields. Places active collection
ID in bibliographic record.

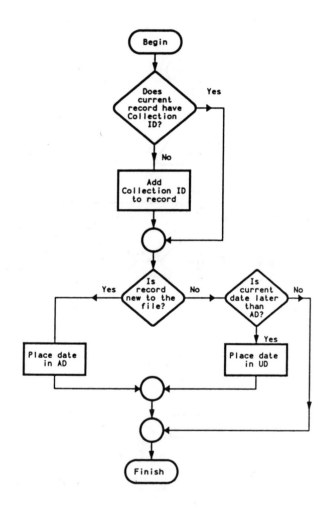

Flowchart 10: BIB Window Post-Save Record

Run after record has been written to file, but before
returning control to user. Updates collection record
and clears system variable BIBID.

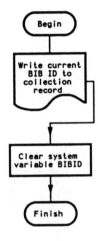

Flowchart 11: ITEM Window Overview

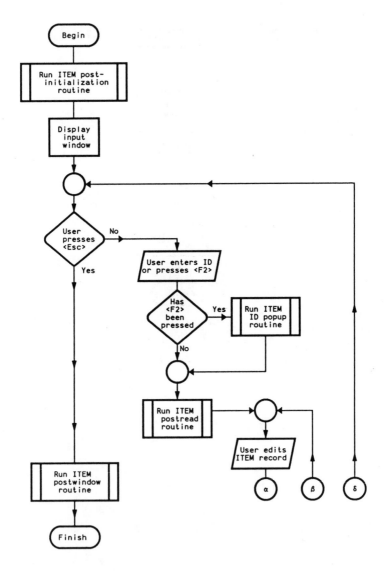

Flowchart 11 *(continued)*

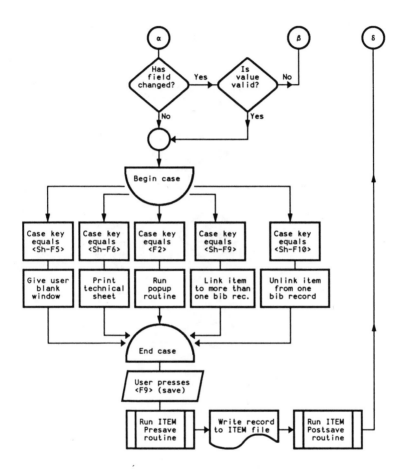

Flowchart 12: ITEM Window Post-Initialization

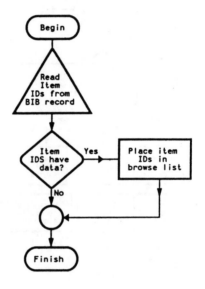

Run when user first accesses ITEM window. Places item IDs
from BIB record in active browse list.

Flowchart 13: ITEM Window ID Popup

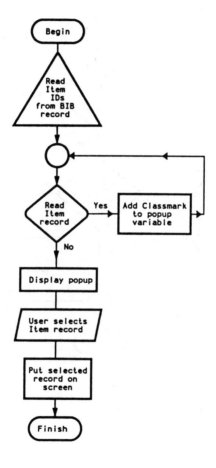

Flowchart 14: ITEM Window Post-Read Record

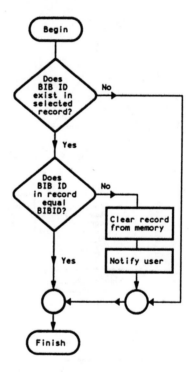

Run after user selects an ITEM record and before the
record displays on screen. Verifies that chosen
record is part of active BIB record.

Flowchart 15: ITEM Window Pre-Prompt Routine

Run when user moves from field to field. Determines default value
(if any) of field, based on kind of material. SAVEFLD is set by
the Item presave routine, which establishes the previously-saved
item record's values as defaults.

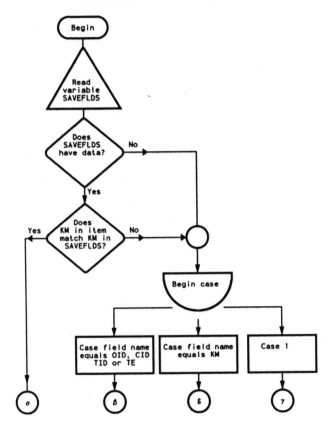

Flowchart 15 *(continued)*

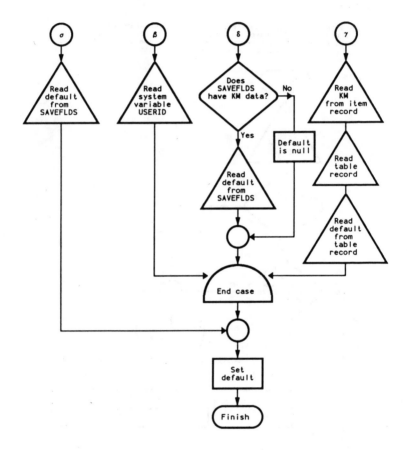

Flowchart 16: ITEM Window Post-Prompt Subroutine

Run when user leaves fields in ITEM window. Determines appropriate
  values for a given field, based on kind of material value, and
    displays popup for user if an incorrect value was input.

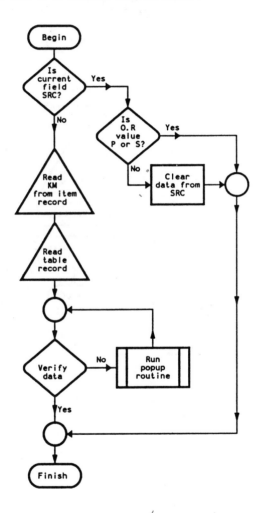

Flowchart 17: ITEM Window Generic Popup Subroutine

Run when user presses <F2> at fields in ITEM window. Determines
appropriate values for a given field, based on kind of material
value, and displays popup for user to select correct setting.
Also run automatically if user inputs an invalid code.

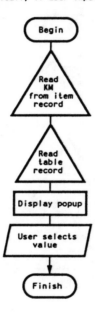

Flowchart 18: ITEM Window Multi-Bib Routine

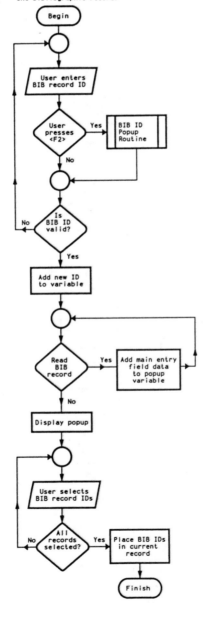

Run when user wants to link one physical item with more than one bibliographic record.

Flowchart 19: ITEM Window Unlink Routine

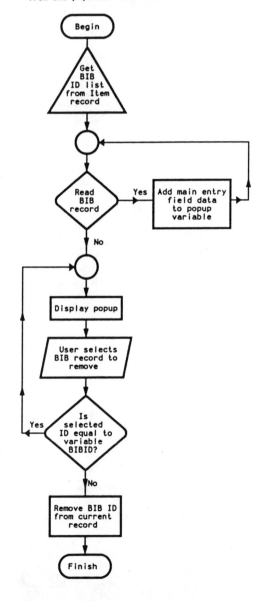

Flowchart 20: ITEM Window Contents Popup

Run when user wants to add contents information to current
  physical item. First retrieves contents in all linked
BIB records, then displays contents for user to select.

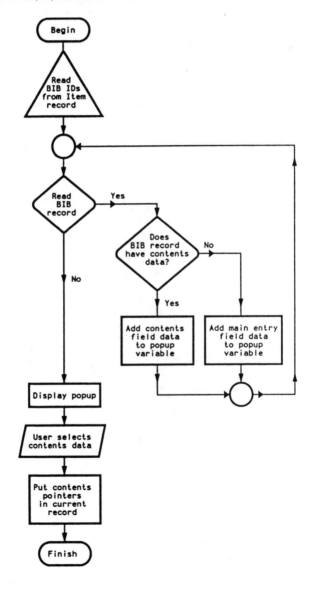

Flowchart 21: ITEM Window Transfer Source Popup

Run when user wants to see the classmarks of original items
linked to BIB record(s) linked to current transfer item.
Depending on the O.R value in the current record, displays
classmarks for original item (for preservation copies), or
preservation item (for service copies) classmarks.

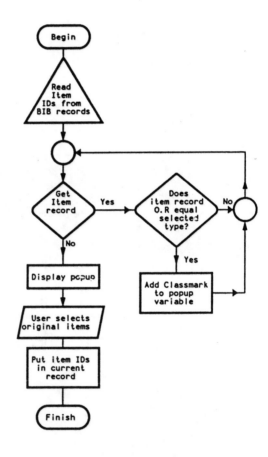

Flowchart 22: ITEM Window Preamp Subroutine

Run when user wants to add phono preamp data to original
item records while describing the preservation copy.

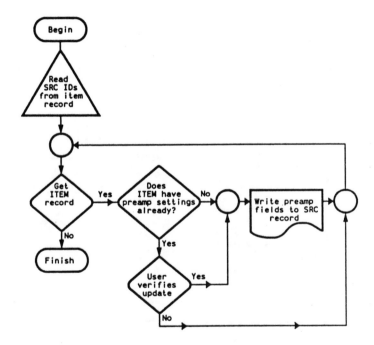

Flowchart 23: Item Record Pre-Save Routine

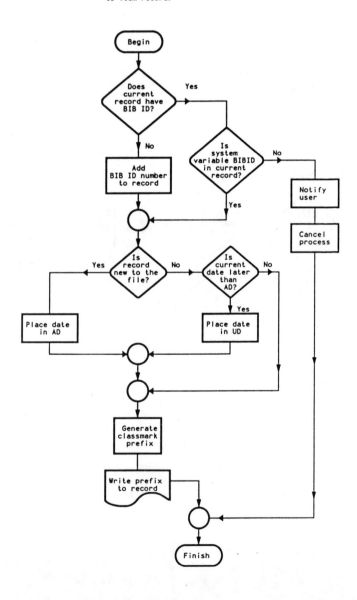

Run after user presses <F9>, but before record is
written to disk. Adds BIB ID to item record. Maintains
Add date and Update date fields. Adds classmark prefix
to item record.

Flowchart 24: ITEM Window Post-Save Record

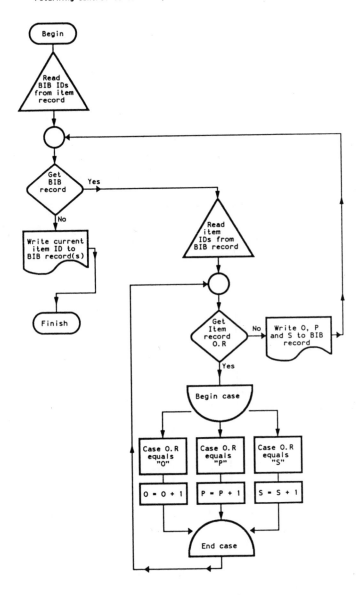

Run after record has been written to file, but before
returning control to user. Updates BIB record(s).

Flowchart 25: ITEM Window Post-Delete Record

Run after record has been deleted from file, but before
returning control to user. Updates BIB record(s).

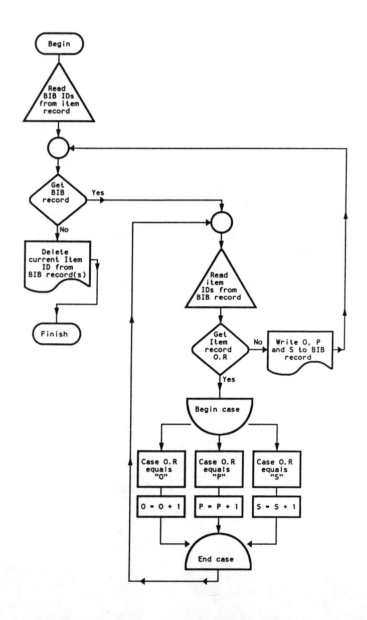

Index